HEILONGJIANG

o Harbin

JILIN

INNER MONGOLIA REGION

Shenyang
LIAONING

NORTH KOREA

SOUTH KOREA

JAPAN

NINGXIA

SHAANXI

SHANXI

HEBEI

o Peking

o Tianjin

SHANDONG

Huang He
(Yellow River)

JIANGSU

o Xian

HENAN

Nanking

o Shanghai

U A N

HUBEI

ANHUI

Chengdu

Wuhan o

Chang Jiang (Yangtze)

ZHEJIANG

qing o

Changsha o

JIANGXI

HUNAN

GUIZHOU

FUJIAN

Taipeh

TAIWAN o

GUANGXI

GUANGDONG

o Guangzhou

HONG KONG

VETNAM

China

HAINAN

LONGMAN GROUP LIMITED
Longman House
Burnt Mill, Harlow, Essex, UK

Produced by Cameron & Tayleur (Books) Ltd.,
25 Lloyd Baker Street, London WC1X 9AT

First published 1981

Printed in Belgium
by Fabrieken Brepols n.v, Turnhout
Setting by Input Typesetting Ltd., London
Reproduction by Tenreck Ltd, London

Series editors: Ian Cameron, Jill Hollis
Designed by Ian Cameron

British Library Cataloguing in Publication Data

Kolpas, Norman
    Mao Tse-tung.—(Longman great lives; 1).
    1. Mao Tse-tung—Juvenile literature
    2. Heads of state—China—Biography
    —Juvenile literature
951.05'092'4   DS778.M3

ISBN 0-582-39032-X

Frontispiece: Mao in
the 1970s.

Picture credits
Anglo-Chinese Educational Institute Library: 8; 20;
    40; 60b; 63b; 64; 67b, c
BBC Hulton Picture Library: 17; 19a; 30b; 32; 35a;
    46b, c; 47a
René Burri, Magnum, New York (John Hillelson
    Agency): 22; 25a
Camera Press: 53; 60c; 61; 63c; 65b; 65c
Cameron & Tayleur: 9; 11; 19b; 21; 23; 24; 25b, c;
    29a, b; 30a; 33a, b; 35c; 36; 37; 38; 39a, b; 45;
    46a; 50a, c; 52a, b; 54; 55b; 57; 60a; 62a, b; 63a
Cooper-Bridgeman Library: 6
Mary Evans Picture Library: 12; 57; 58
Imperial War Museum, London: 27
Keystone Press Agency: 50a; 62c
The Mansell Collection: 7
Popperfoto: 31; 34; 35b; 42; 47b; 48a, b; 49; 55a; 56;
    59a; 65a; 66; 67a
Salamander Books Limited: 34a
Sovfoto Agency, New York: 44
The Sunday Times: 5
Wayland Picture Library: 43
Jack Wilkes © Life Magazine: 51

Maps by Creative Cartography Ltd. (Terry Allen and
Nicholas Skelton).

Cameron & Tayleur wish to thank the China
Philatelic Society and Elizabeth Wright of The Great
Britain-China Centre for their help in the preparation
of this book.

Contents

1. Mao's Early Years   6
2. Mao Gains an Education   16
3. The Communist Party   26
4. Wilderness and War   36
5. Turmoil and Triumph   46
6. Mao's China   54
Chronology Index
Books to Read   68

The Chinese language does not use the English alphabet but has its own set of characters. For books in English, the Chinese sounds have to be turned into English letters by a process called transliteration. Unfortunately, this can be done in a number of ways, and the system which has been used for many years is being replaced by a new one called Pinyin. At present, Pinyin is being used for all except the most famous names, which are spelled in the old way. We have used Pinyin in this book for most names, with the following exceptions (Pinyin spellings in brackets): people – Mao Tse-tung [Mao Zedong], Chou En-lai [Zhou Enlai], Chiang Kai-shek [Jiang Jieshi], Sun Yat-sen [Sun Zhongshan]; cities – Peking [Beijing], Nanking [Nanjing]; river – Yangtze [Chang Jiang]. Note that "x" is pronounced "sh", and "zh" sounds like "j".

Mao

NORMAN KOLPAS

Longman

1.   Mao's Early Years

"For thousands of years the several hundred million Chinese people have all led the life of slaves. Only one person, the Emperor, was not a slave, and even he could be called the slave of 'heaven'."

These words were written in 1919 by Mao Tse-tung, a farmer's son from the central Chinese province of Hunan, who completely changed the lives of the 800 million Chinese, about one-fifth of the world's population.

For over 3,000 years, China had been ruled by all-powerful emperors who believed they were the Sons of Heaven, sent to earth with divine authority to control its central land – the great "Middle Kingdom" of China. The Emperors were aided by a small class of wealthy and well-educated administrators who collected the taxes, enforced the laws, and raised armies to defend their vast country.

Under the rule of the Emperors and their assistants, the commerce, science and culture of China flourished. Almost

China had been producing fine works of art for much more than a thousand years when this beautiful watercolour was painted. It dates from the Ming dynasty of Emperors (1368–1644).

The aged Dowager Empress Ci Xi, who was the effective ruler of China from 1898 to 1908.

a thousand years ago, Chinese ships traded with India and the Philippines, and a little later they visited the eastern shores of Africa. Chinese inventors were responsible for gunpowder, paper, the compass and printing with movable type. Chinese writers produced sensitive poetry and epic tales. From ancient China came exquisite works in silk and porcelain (two more Chinese discoveries), sculpture and painting; their simple beauty still seems fresh and exciting.

The serenity and perfection of Chinese arts were inspired, as were all things in China, by traditional religious and philosophical teachings. The writings of the philosopher Confucius, who lived about 500 years before Christ, taught people that true happiness came only from knowing and obediently accepting the place in society which had been ordained for them by Heaven.

The life ordained for the Son of Heaven and his ruling class was made comfortable by the luxuries of wealth and the beauties of art. But the great majority of the Chinese people, the peasants who scratched a living from the land, were condemned from birth to hardship and poverty.

Mao Tse-tung was himself the son of a peasant. He was born on 26th December 1893 in Shaoshan, a small village in a mountain valley 65 km. (40 miles) south of Changsha, the capital city of Hunan Province. Mao's father was Mao Rensheng (in Chinese, the family name comes first). The son of a poor peasant, Mao Rensheng had two years' schooling as a boy. As a young man, he was forced to serve in the army to help pay his father's debts. When Mao Rensheng finally paid off the debts, he returned to Shaoshan. By living frugally and saving carefully, he was able to buy a small piece of rice farmland, some of it land lost by his father. With success, he gradually increased this and began to trade in a small way in the transport and sale of grain.

Mao Rensheng was now a "rich peasant", but the life he and his family led was anything but luxurious. They lived in a house that had originally been built by Mao Rensheng's father in 1878. It was a mud-walled bungalow with a low thatched roof and earthen floors. Mao Rensheng enlarged it, building two wings on either side of the main central room. On one side were the Maos; on the other lived an entirely separate family, the Zous. The central living room, open to both families, was split straight down the middle. Later, when Mao Rensheng decided to tile the roof, the Zous' side remained thatched. The rooms had few pieces of furniture, and strings of hot red peppers, a speciality of

Hunan, festooned the roof beams, from which they hung for storage.

Even toddlers in Hunan were taught to eat these fiery peppers. They nibbled on them habitually, much as we might chew gum. Young Mao Tse-tung was particularly fond of peppers. In fact, they were all that gave interest to his daily meals. His father allowed him and the rest of the family only rice and some home-grown vegetables for their breakfast, lunch and supper, while the hired farmhands (one all the year and a second for the rice harvest) were given a bit of egg or meat with their meals once a month.

Young Mao Tse-tung had no time for play. As a tiny child he stayed close to his mother, while she did her share of the farm work. He also went with her on her occasional visits to Buddhist religious ceremonies, a practice that was disliked by his father, who was not a believer, but managed nevertheless to tolerate a large bronze statue of Buddha near the entrance to their house.

When Mao Tse-tung was six years old, his father made him start taking a full part in the work of the farm. Every morning, Mao rose before the sun to attend to his chores. He cleaned the pigsties and cared for the family's work

The house occupied by the Maos and the Zous at Shaoshan, now a museum, but still tiled at the Mao end and thatched at the Zou end.

8

animal, a buffalo. In the fields, he helped with planting rice, weeding, and gathering the harvest. Strangest of all his tasks, young Mao, a frail and scrawny lad, sometimes played the role of scarecrow, sitting on a platform in the middle of the fields and waving his arms to drive away the birds.

If Mao Rensheng caught his son loafing, he beat him severely. He was an old-fashioned father, who expected his children to be unquestioningly obedient. Mao Tse-tung, his two younger brothers and their adopted sister all learned to fear their father.

They loved their mother, Wen Jimei, deeply. She was an illiterate peasant, a simple woman, whose large eyes, thick hair and warm smile could be seen reflected in her children's features. Her finest trait, and the most irritating to her husband, was her charity. "My mother was a kind woman," said Mao Tse-tung, "generous and sympathetic and always ready to share what she had. She pitied the poor and often gave them rice when they came to ask for it during famines. But she could not do so when my father was present."

Wen Jimei did this because of her deep religious piety. Although young Mao soon left behind his own religious beliefs, he never forgot his mother's most important

The kitchen of the house at Shaoshan.

9

lesson. She taught him, from an early age, that he had a responsibility towards the poor people of China.

When Mao Tse-tung was eight, his father decided that he should have a traditional education. Learning to write in the style of a scholar educated in the writings of Confucius might give the boy a chance to become a civil servant and pull his family, well off though they may have been, out of the ranks of the lowly peasant class. At the very least, Mao Rensheng thought, an education would enable the boy to help with the business: he could keep the books and use cleverly chosen quotations from Confucius to defeat rival merchants in the occasional lawsuit.

Mao Tse-tung was enrolled at the local village primary school. Each morning, he had to hurry through his usual farm jobs before going off to a full day's schooling. In the evening, he returned home for more physical work and, as his knowledge increased, additional business tasks.

The school was old-fashioned, run by an aged teacher who, Mao said, "belonged to the stern-treatment school." Mao learned to recite the sayings of Confucius by heart, but he quickly began to turn his conservative education to the ways of modern rebellion. Now, when his father commanded him to pay respect and work hard, as Confucius said he must, young Mao replied that the ancient philosopher also taught that older people should be "kind and affectionate" and capable of doing more physical work than the young.

Mao Tse-tung also brought his rebellion into the schoolroom. Each student was expected, in turn, to stand up in front of the teacher's desk and recite a lesson to the class. One day, when Mao's turn came as usual, he refused to leave his desk, saying that everyone could hear him just as well if he stayed where he sat. The teacher, mad with rage, tried to pull Mao from his seat, but the boy resisted, holding on with all his might. Finally, Mao ran from the schoolroom.

Terrified of going home and certain that his father would give him the beating of his life, Mao decided to run away to the city, to the provincial capital, Changsha. For three days he wandered through the hills, lost. When his parents finally found him, Mao was embarrassed to learn that he had been walking in circles and had never been more than 4.5 km (3 miles) from home.

Surprisingly, after this incident, Mao received kinder treatment from both his father and the teacher. He later recalled the incident as "a successful 'strike'."

Mao continued to rebel, but in a more ordinary way. Like his fellow pupils, he read exciting old Chinese adventure stories when he should have been studying the classics.

Mao's favourites were tales of revolution and rebellion, including *The Water Margin* (which has been translated into English as *All Men Are Brothers* by Pearl Buck) and other books that had been banned a hundred years before by the Manchu dynasty of emperors. The plot of *The Water Margin*, a Chinese equivalent of the Robin Hood legend, makes it clear why the Manchus disliked these books: a band of 108 outcast warriors fight bloody battles against an evil emperor and his court, trying to right the wrongs done to the peasants by their harsh rulers.

Pretending to be intent on their studies, Mao and the other children memorized these stories. On their way to and from school each day, they would swap their favourite episodes with the old men of the village. However, the teacher, who thought the books wicked, attempted to confiscate them whenever he could. Mao had to cover the window and doorway of his room at night with blankets to prevent his disapproving father from seeing the flickering of the oil lamp by which he read the outlawed stories.

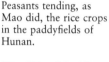
Peasants tending, as Mao did, the rice crops in the paddyfields of Hunan.

In 1906, when Mao was thirteen, his father made him leave the village school to work full time on the farm, "doing the full labour of a man during the day and at night keeping

11

A Japanese attack during the Sino-Japanese War of 1894.

books for my father." But Mao was strong and rapidly growing towards the six-foot height he would eventually attain. Already he could carry two large, heavy baskets of manure, slung on a pole across his shoulders, when he went out to the fields.

Mao always believed in strenuous exercise. Even as a boy, he built up his strength by exercising daily. He taught himself to swim in the two lotus ponds on the farm and he loved to go for long hikes among the surrounding mountains.

Every day, when he went out into the fields, Mao took copies of his favourite books. He hurried through his morning work, carrying fifteen basketloads of manure from the house. Then he could settle down behind a nearby tomb, in the shade of a huge tree, and read his books until lunchtime. Every afternoon, he repeated his pattern of work and study until supper time.

In addition to his boyhood favourites, Mao now began to read more serious books, which dealt with the problems of China. One, called *Words of Warning*, told him of modern China's weakness in comparison with other nations, the cause of which, he read, was "her lack of Western appliances – railways, telephones, telegraphs, and steamships."

China in trouble

By this time, China had been exposed to influences from Europe, largely against her will, for over a hundred years. Since the 18th century, silk and porcelain, cotton and tea, had been exported on a large scale to Britain, at first in return for gold and silver. No other payment would satisfy the Chinese until the British East India Company discovered

12

that China could offer a huge market for the addictive drug opium, which it cultivated in India. Soon, the Chinese were paying gold and silver for opium. The Chinese merchants grew rich, while the opium smoke dulled the suffering and also the ambition of the lower classes.

Both the British government and the Chinese merchants resisted attempts by the Chinese authorities to ban the opium trade or to confine it to Hong Kong, on the southeastern coast of China. In 1839, war broke out when the Chinese burned some British cargoes of opium. After the defeat of China, the Treaty of Nanking in 1842 gave Hong Kong to the British and opened the rest of the country to foreign trade. Further humiliations at the hands of the world's great trading nations culminated in 1899 when the United States, fearing unfair competition from other countries, declared an "Open Door Policy", which guaranteed trade with China for all.

But perhaps the worst blow of all to Chinese national pride came in 1894, when Mao Tse-tung was less than a year old. War broke out with Japan over possession of the Korean peninsula. The Chinese fleet was routed by the Japanese, a people the Chinese had always considered to be an inferior race of *woren*, or "dwarves". Money that should have paid for more ships to defend China was instead spent by the Emperor on restoring his palace in the capital, Peking. The victorious Japanese took control of the island of Taiwan and part of Manchuria.

Throughout China, disorganized rebellion started breaking out against both the foreigners and the Manchu emperors. Mao Tse-tung's teenage years were spent in a climate of rising unrest. Even though there was no radio or television and he had not yet seen a newspaper, the young man learned of the tensions in China through the daily events in his village and conversation with passing strangers.

Several years of desperately poor harvests had brought Hunan Province to the edge of famine. Poor people could not get enough food, while merchants hoarded their supplies to sell to the more wealthy. In Changsha, the starving peasants demanded food from the Governor. His reply, as Mao remembered from hearing of the event, was "Why haven't you food? There is plenty in the city. I always have enough."

The poor rioted and drove the Governor away, but the Emperor quickly sent a successor, who had the peasant leaders executed. Their heads were stuck on poles and displayed in public as a warning.

In Mao's village, Shaoshan, poor villagers seized shipments of rice from wealthier farmers and merchants, including Mao Rensheng. Mao Tse-tung sympathized with their actions. He was also thrilled by stories of a secret society called Ge Lao Hui, which had violently opposed the Emperor. In Shaoshan, the society was taken to court in a land dispute with a local landlord. Because of his money and connections, the landlord was able to defeat the Ge Lao Hui. But they refused to accept the word of the court, even when government troops were called out. They fled to a nearby mountain, where they built up defences and waged battle before finally being overpowered.

Mao leaves home

Mao Tse-tung was impressed by the heroism of these peasants. The events made him slowly realize something about the books he loved, such as *The Water Margin*. Although they told of men who fought bravely for justice and right, "all the characters were warriors, officials or scholars; there was never a peasant hero ... all glorified men of arms, rulers of the people, who did not have to work the land,

Map of Hunan Province.

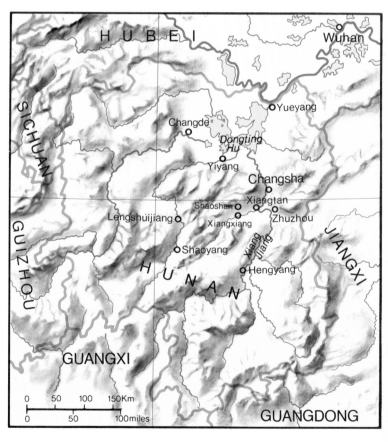

because they owned and controlled it and evidently made the peasants work it for them."

Mao had long talks with a local schoolteacher, a "radical" who believed that religion was deceiving the people. The teacher wanted all the temples to be shut down and changed into schools teaching useful things. Mao agreed with him.

Mao was still only 15 years old. He wanted to return to school to further his studies and search for a solution to China's problems. But his father wanted him to settle down, marry and have children.

According to custom, a marriage was arranged between Mao Tse-tung and a village girl who was some five years older. Old Mao forced his son to take part in the wedding ceremony but Mao Tse-tung would not live with his bride, and the marriage was soon declared to be broken, much to the shame of the bride's family. To this day, out of sympathy for their feelings, no one in Shaoshan will disclose the family's name.

Still wanting to learn, Mao ran away to live and study with a law student in the town of Xiangdan. This politically active young man introduced Mao to other young radical thinkers who wanted to change China. Mao read continuously and spent the nights talking and arguing until the small hours with his new friends.

After six months, Mao Rensheng summoned his son back home. He had made arrangements to apprentice his son to a friend of his, a rice merchant.

Mao at first liked the idea of earning his own living. But then a young relative came to Shaoshan on a visit, and told him about a new school in his town of Xiangxiang, which offered boys the chance to acquire the "new knowledge" of Western ways.

Mao Tse-tung knew he had to go there. He argued long and fiercely with his father, who thought the school would do the boy no good. Finally, friends of his father convinced old Mao that his son could earn much more money if he had an advanced education. Mao Rensheng finally consented.

So, one morning in 1910, the 16-year-old Mao Tse-tung gathered together two tattered bed sheets, some worn and faded tunics, a mosquito net and his dog-eared adventure books. He tied these few possessions in a bundle, bid his mother a fond goodbye and, without a word to his father, set out to walk about 30 km (almost 20 miles) to his new life in Xiangxiang.

2. Mao Gains an Education

The Dongshan School in Xiangxiang occupied a large house on the outskirts of the town. The building and schoolyard were surrounded by a high stone wall, which was encircled by a wide moat filled with golden carp. To Mao, who was used to his tiny village schoolroom, Dongshan looked like a fortress.

On the road to Xiangxiang he met a small boy who was a student at a neighbouring school. When Mao told him that he was to be a student at Dongshan, the boy appeared surprised and amused. Mao soon found out why.

He had never seen so many children in one place before, and not one of them was more than 12 years old. Most were the sons of wealthy landlords and wore expensive clothing decorated with brocade. They all laughed at the tall, awkward 16-year-old peasant who spoke with the accent of another region and wore a tattered coat and trousers made from coarse blue cloth.

Mao worked hard to catch up with these younger, better-educated boys, who soon grew to respect him. He was particularly good at essay writing, and received top marks even though his handwriting was large and clumsy. In his free time, Mao continued to study even harder, searching for knowledge of his country and the world beyond.

He became friends with the school's music and English teacher, who was despised by the other students and was nicknamed "False Foreign Devil". At the time, all Chinese men and boys wore pigtails, or *queues*, as required by the teachings of Confucius and the edicts of the emperors. Although he was Chinese, False Foreign Devil had studied in Japan and cut off his *queue* while abroad; at Dongshan, he wore a false pigtail. Mao, unworried by his obvious strangeness, loved to hear him talk about Japan and her growing strength and pride.

Mao's passion for reading continued. A cousin of his sent him books by two intellectuals who had tried twelve years before to encourage the Emperor to reform the country's schools, courts, army and other institutions. Mao read their works again and again. And from a fellow student he borrowed a book called *Great Heroes of the World*, which included the lives of such men as Washington, Napoleon, Wellington and Lincoln. When Mao returned the book, he had to apologize. He had been so excited by the achievements of these leaders that, without thinking, he had marked the passages that interested him most. Mao believed from his reading that China's salvation depended on great men coming forth to serve and advise the Emperor.

Changsha

After half a year at Dongshan, Mao grew tired of the school and of lessons he now found to be simple and childish. He applied to attend a Middle School in the provincial capital of Changsha and, to his surprise, was accepted. In September 1911, he travelled by steamboat up the Xiang River to the bustling city of Changsha.

Shortly after his arrival, Mao discovered an exciting new sort of reading matter: his first newspaper. His excitement was overshadowed by the news he read, for the paper was *People's Strength*, the official journal of the United League, headed by Dr. Sun Yat-sen, the leading figure in the struggle against the Manchu government.

In *People's Strength*, Mao read news of local uprisings throughout China by the common people against their

Dr. Sun Yat-sen, photographed after his return from exile, at Nanking in February 1912.

rulers, and editorials demanding an end to imperial rule and the establishment of a true democracy. Mao was so inspired that he wrote a political article himself, suggesting that Sun Yat-sen, who was at that time in exile, raising support for his cause in Japan, Europe and the United States, should be made president of a new Chinese Republic. Mao posted his article on the wall of his school, just as other Chinese thinkers had publicly posted their protests and demands for over three thousand years.

To show that they were no longer the Emperor's subjects, Mao and some fellow students made a pact to cut off their *queues*. However, only Mao and one other student lived up to their pledges. Rather than let the others go back on their words, Mao and his comrade "assaulted them in secret and forcibly removed their *queues*, a total of more than ten falling victim to our shears."

All over China, supporters of Sun Yat-sen were ready for far more significant actions. On 9th October 1911, in the city of Hankou, in Hubei Province, 320 km (200 miles) northeast of Changsha, a group of young officers in the Imperial Army, who were secret members of Sun's United League, accidentally exploded a bomb. Their mutinous plot was immediately discovered, and they were executed that day. But the following day, 10th October, just across the Yangtze River in the city of Wuchang, the officers of another garrison led a successful revolt inspired by their dead comrades. Over the next two months, province after province was won by Sun Yat-sen's people, and on 29th December 1911, Dr. Sun returned to China and was declared its President.

Having decided to join the revolutionary troops who were going to take Changsha, Mao realized that he would need a good pair of waterproof shoes. It was, after all, the rainy season. A friend had a spare pair to lend. But as Mao left the city to collect the shoes, he was stopped by government soldiers as a suspicious character. While they questioned him, the troops guarding the city decided to join Dr. Sun's United League; by the time Mao was released, Changsha had fallen.

The sweetness of victory in Changsha and elsewhere soon went sour. A new Governor and Vice-Governor were elected, both from among the poor of the city. They tried immediately to reform the life of Changsha. The richer men of the city, landlords and merchants who had also supported the revolution, were afraid that some of their wealth might

Imperial forces at the front during the revolution in early 1912.

Stamps issued in 1912 to celebrate the revolution and the founding of the Chinese republic, bearing the portraits of Sun Yat-sen and Yuan Shikai respectively.

be confiscated. They decided to do away with their new officials. Not many days later, Mao saw their corpses lying in the street.

In northern China, Imperial troops led by the army chief of staff Yuan Shikai continued to resist the United League forces. Their military might was far greater than that of the revolutionaries. There was a great call for students to join the fight for the Republic against Yuan and the Emperor's supporters. Mao answered the call.

He could have joined the student army, but he considered them to be "too confused". So Mao applied to join the regular army, which was now on the side of the Republic. Being six feet tall, taller than most Chinese men, he was readily accepted.

He saw no action, but put his six months in the army to good use. While most of the soldiers spent their pay on drink, food and entertainment, Mao spent only a third of his pay on food and water. The rest went on newspapers, of which he became an avid reader.

In one of them, the *Xiang River Daily News*, he read for the first time about socialism, the political system in which, ideally, the workers control their fields, their factories and their government. Mao enthusiastically discussed with the other soldiers in his squad the possibility of making China a socialist country.

By January 1912, Sun Yat-sen had realized that continued fighting could only weaken the country and ultimately lead to his defeat. He therefore proposed by telegram that if General Yuan Shikai forced the Emperor to abdicate, he could take over the title of President. Yuan agreed and became President in February. Peace was restored for a while, and Mao left the army.

Mao knew he wanted to study. But what? Every newspaper carried appealing advertisements for new schools. First he applied for a police school; before taking the entrance examination, however, he saw another advertisement for a school that taught soap-making. It told of the great social benefits of soap-making, and how it would enrich the country and the people. Mao applied to join.

His enthusiasm for soap-making was soon followed by an even greater zeal for the legal profession. Then a friend talked Mao into applying for commercial school. Mao stayed for only a month. All the instruction was in English, and Mao knew "scarcely more than the alphabet." This fiasco was followed by six months at the Changsha First Provincial Middle School, which Mao left because he found it too strict and formal.

Finally, he decided that he might be better off simply educating himself. Every morning, he went to the Hunan Provincial Library at opening time. Pausing only at midday for a quick lunch of two rice cakes, he sat in the library and read until closing time. He read translations of Adam Smith's classic study of economics, *The Wealth of Nations*, and Charles Darwin's treatise on evolution, *The Origin of Species*, books on philosophy, world history and geography, as well as poetry and romances. Whenever Mao read about some new place, he memorized its position on a large map on the library wall, the first map of the world he had ever seen.

The First Normal School of Hunan in Changsha, the teacher training college where Mao was a student from 1913 to 1918.

Mao Tse-tung found the library an ideal place to study. After six months, however, his father could no longer agree to this idea of self-education. He threatened to cut off the

Mao in 1914.

small allowance that bought his son food and lodgings in a boarding house crowded with soldiers and students. Fortunately, before he became penniless, Mao discovered the advertisement that was to solve all his problems:

First Normal School of Hunan
Tuition and Board Free
Educational Work after Graduation
Education Lays the Foundation of a Country

If learning and education were of highest importance to Mao, then perhaps he could serve others by helping them to learn as well. Mao decided to enrol in the First Normal School, the teacher training college in Changsha.

Mao remained at the First Normal School for five years. His courses covered literature, social sciences, natural sciences and art, the subject that he liked least: "I thought it extremely stupid. I used to think of the simplest subjects possible to draw, finish up quickly and leave the class." During one art exam, Mao drew an oval on a clean sheet of paper, and labelled it "egg". He failed, with a mark of 40 per cent.

In the classes that really mattered to him at the school, Mao excelled. He was best at ethics, the study of moral standards. It was taught by Yang Changzhi, a professor who had studied philosophy in England, who "tried to imbue his students with the desire to become just, moral, virtuous men, useful in society." Mao's essays for Yang received top marks; one entitled "The Energy of the Mind", was given the maximum mark of 100, plus an extra five points for superior effort.

Yang Changzhi often invited his students home to dine with him and his wife and children. So Mao became acquainted with Yang's shy and intelligent young daughter, Kaihui.

Yang instilled in Mao and his other students an enthusiasm for a spartan life-style, which agreed with Mao's already strong belief in physical fitness. "In the winter holidays we tramped through the fields, up and down mountains, along city walls, and across the streams and rivers. If it rained we took off our shirts and called it a rain bath. When the sun was hot we also doffed shirts and called it a sun bath. In the spring winds, we shouted that this was a new sport called 'wind bathing'. We slept in the open when frost was already falling and even in November swam in the cold rivers." During two summer holidays, Mao and a fellow

Mao (third from left) with fellow students of the First Normal College, around 1917.

student even lived as beggars, hiking across the countryside and relying on their own wits, and the kindness and charity of others, for food and lodging.

Yang's students knew they might soon have to fight as soldiers. The political compromise between Sun Yat-sen and Yuan Shikai had been short-lived. While Yuan openly assured Sun that they were still on the same side, he was methodically assassinating and executing Sun's followers, members of the United League, which had now been renamed the Guomindang Party, and replacing them in the National Assembly with his own men.

During the last months of 1913 and the beginning of 1914, rich generals, commanding their own forces, began to fight each other for control of provinces or regions; these "warlords" gradually eroded Yuan's power. China could get no help from outside to stabilize the situation; in August 1914, World War I had begun, and all the resources of Europe and America were needed for their own battles.

In 1915, Japan, seeing China's increasing weakness, presented Yuan with a list of 21 demands, which would put the country largely under Japanese control. Desperate to stay in power at any price, Yuan conceded, and crowned himself Emperor in December 1915. Six months later, he died of a heart attack, leaving China to the warlords and the Japanese. By the middle of 1917, two unsteady warlord coalitions had been formed: the northern warlords, based in Peking, and the warlords of the south, based in Guangzhou, who chose Sun Yat-sen as their leader. Neither side was strong enough, however, to resist increasing Japanese influence over their country.

By this time, Mao Tse-tung's studies and thoughts were beginning to focus sharply on his country's situation. In April 1917, Mao wrote his first published article, for the magazine *New Youth*, to which he had been introduced by his teacher, Yang. The article, called "A Study of Physical Culture", set out a personal fitness programme for Mao's countrymen to follow. "The principal aim of physical education," he wrote, "is military heroism."

Mao also "inserted an advertisement in a Changsha paper inviting young men interested in patriotic work to make contact with me. I specified youths who were hardened and determined, and ready to make sacrifices for their country." This daunting advertisement received only a few responses, but little by little Mao attracted more young men to his

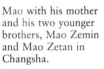

Mao with his mother and his two younger brothers, Mao Zemin and Mao Zetan in Changsha.

"serious-minded little group"; it ultimately grew to 70 or 80 members and took on the title of New People's Study Society. They talked "only of large matters – the nature of men, of human society, of China, the world and the universe." But still Mao and the others were uncertain of precisely what direction they, and China, should take.

Mao graduated from the First Normal School of Changsha in 1918. During his final year, his mother died, and so Mao had no desire to return to live in Shaoshan.

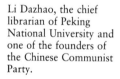
Mao goes to Peking

In Changsha, Mao had helped to set up a scheme by which the French government would bring Chinese students to France for work and study. Before the students of Hunan left for France, they planned to study French in the northern capital, Peking. Mao himself did not wish to visit France: "I felt that I did not know enough about my own country, and that my time could be more profitably spent in China." Still, Mao went with his fellow students to Peking, his first visit to northern China.

His favourite teacher, Yang Changzhi, was now a professor at Peking National University. With his help, Mao found

Li Dazhao, the chief librarian of Peking National University and one of the founders of the Chinese Communist Party.

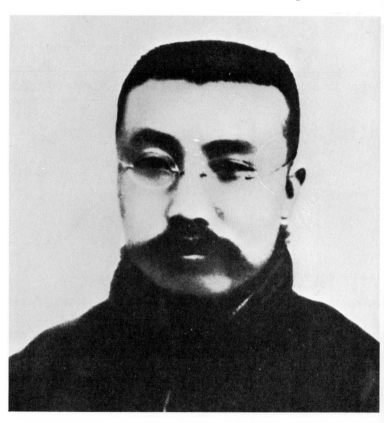

Mao Tse-tung's father, Mao Rensheng, around 1917.

Yang Kaihui, the daughter of Mao's favourite teacher in Changsha.

Chinese communism acknowledges its debt to Karl Marx: a stamp issued in 1957.

work there as an assistant to the chief librarian, Li Dazhao. It was such a lowly job that people avoided him. "One of my tasks was to register the names of people who came to read newspapers, but to most of them I didn't exist as a human being." He tried to converse with the scholars, "but they were very busy men. They had no time to listen to an assistant librarian speaking southern dialect."

Mao's living conditions were even less heartening than his job. He found quarters in a boarding house, sharing a single room with seven others. They all slept on a large bed, a *kang*, made of bricks and warmed from beneath by a fire. At night, Mao said, "I used to have to warn people on each side of me when I wanted to turn over." Between the seven of them, they owned at first only one, and finally three, coats; Mao, who did not own one himself, had to wait his turn to borrow a coat if he wanted to go out on really cold days.

Mao found compensation for this hard life in the beauties of Peking, in wandering through its parks and the grounds of its old imperial palace. His thoughts on these walks turned to classical poetry. They also turned to romance. In the library, he again met Yang's daughter, Kaihui, who was now a student at the university. They fell in love.

Mao's job in the library also meant that he had access to journals, books and maps, so that he could continue his studies. He was able to join student societies of philosophy and journalism and to attend some classes. Most important, Mao was invited to join an informal study group headed by his boss, Li Dazhao. Its subject was Marxism, the political and social theories of the German philosopher Karl Marx.

Marx's teachings were particularly topical at that time. Just a year before, in October 1917, a communist revolution had taken place in Russia. Marx had taught that every society based on capitalism, in which the factories and farms were owned by a small wealthy class, contained the seeds of its own destruction in the downtrodden masses of poor people who could only make a living by working for the rich. Violent revolution by the poor, Marx had asserted, was the only way to overthrow a capitalist state and set up the equality-for-all system of socialism or communism.

During the winter of 1918–19, Mao came to believe strongly that Marx's theories offered the solution to China's problems. Although there was not yet an official Communist Party in China, Mao himself was rapidly becoming a communist.

3. The Communist Party

At the beginning of April 1919, Mao set off with his Hunanese friends on the 1,100 km (700 mile) journey southeast to the bustling port city of Shanghai, to bid them farewell on their voyage to France. Mao's journey was as haphazard as his daily life in Peking had been. All he could afford was a ticket as far as Tianjin, only some 100 km (60 miles) from Peking. At the last minute, however, a companion loaned Mao the money for a ticket to Pukou, more than two-thirds of the distance to Shanghai. In Pukou, Mao, penniless once more, was robbed of his shoes. Again, he was lucky: at the railway station he met an old acquaintance from Hunan, who loaned him enough money to buy new shoes and a ticket to complete the journey. Once in Shanghai, Mao discovered that the money raised to send the students to France included a sum set aside to give him a comfortable journey home to Changsha.

On his trip to Shanghai, Mao had the chance to visit some historic places such as the grave of Confucius at Qufu and the ancient walled city of Xuzhou, a place he had read about as a boy in adventure books. Although Mao looked upon his sightseeing as "achievements worth adding to my adventures", they were also something of a farewell to the past for him; he returned to Hunan ready and eager to take "a more direct role in politics" and to change China by his own efforts.

An unhappy peace

World War I had ended in November 1918, and in January 1919 a conference had been convened at Versailles, on the outskirts of Paris, to decide on terms of peace. Both China and Japan, who had supported the Allied powers in the war, were among the victorious nations who sent delegates to the conference.

There was hope in China that, with the peace treaty, the Western powers would end their interests in Chinese territory, and that China would be able to stand on an equal footing with Japan among the world's nations. But China, still in the grip of civil turmoil, did not have a very strong influence over the decisions made at Versailles. The country was not granted any of its wishes for fair treatment. Worse still, Chinese territories that had once been controlled by the defeated Germans were not returned to China by her allies. They were handed over to Japan.

The people of China were not just humiliated when they learned of this, they were also enraged by the treatment meted out to them by the foreigners and by the way their own warlords had co-operated with the Japanese in their efforts to dominate China. On 4th May 1919, 3,000 students held a demonstration in Peking against the unfair peace treaty and China's corrupt, pro-Japanese leaders. Hundreds of demonstrators were arrested, but support for the Peking students spread quickly across China. Trade unions formed everywhere, as workers joined together to discuss their dissatisfaction. Strikes were called in sympathy and protest. In the city of Shanghai alone, on 6th June, some 90,000 people, including textile workers, waiters, dockers, and policemen, stopped work, bringing the city to a halt.

Spreading the word

In Changsha, Mao Tse-tung played his part in the movement. During the day, he taught in a primary school. Every evening and weekend, however, Mao devoted to political activities. The New People's Study Society, which he had founded as a student, was thriving. Mao brought to it his new-found knowledge of Marxism, and his talks on the subject attracted the city's workers as well as its students.

Mao also founded the *Xiang River Review*, a weekly newspaper that gained immediate popularity with the students of Hunan. Mao was the editor and wrote articles that were stirring, eloquent and yet so simple in their choice of words that even people with the smallest amount of education could understand them. "As soon as we arise and let out a shout," Mao wrote, "the traitors will get up and tremble and flee for their lives."

The signing of the peace treaty in the Hall of Mirrors at the Palace of Versailles, near Paris, on 28th June 1919, from a painting by Sir William Orpen. The central figures are (left to right) Woodrow Wilson for the United States, Georges Clemenceau for France and David Lloyd George for Britain.

One traitor constantly criticized by Mao in his articles was Zhang Jingyao, "a vicious character" who held the post of Governor of Hunan with the support of the warlord in Peking. Mao organized a general student strike against Zhang and sent delegates to Peking and to Sun Yat-sen in southwestern China, asking for help in removing Zhang from office.

Zhang's response was to shut down the *Xiang River Review* and to hire assassins to murder Mao. But before they had their chance, Mao was off to Peking once more.

In January 1920, he arrived in the capital as a correspondent for several Hunan journals, aiming to rally support against Zhang. In this, he failed; the problems of Hunan seemed small and unimportant to the radical intellectuals of the capital. But in a much more important way, he succeeded.

Before in Peking, Mao had been a humble assistant librarian. Now he was the esteemed editor of the *Xiang River Review* and the author of articles that had been greatly admired in the city. A year before, the librarian Li Dazhao had no more than tolerated Mao's presence in his study group; now he asked for Mao's help in setting up a Chinese Communist Party. Mao was now a convinced Marxist, having just read Marx's own words for the first time in a Chinese translation of the *Communist Manifesto*. He agreed to do all that he could to further communism in Hunan.

Mao was supported in his decision by Yang Kaihui. She had also been learning the principles of Marxism in Peking study groups and had taken part in the student demonstrations there on 4th May 1919. She and Mao pledged to work together to build a Chinese revolution. They became engaged to be married.

After two months in Peking, Mao was urged by Li to go to Shanghai, where he would find the influential Chen Duxiu, editor of *New Youth*, the journal for which Mao had written his first published article. During his four months in Shanghai, Mao earned his living by the only job he could find, working 14 hours a day in a laundry, washing clothes and sheets in a hot, steaming basement and delivering huge bundles of clean clothes all over the city. At night, he met with Chen and others in newly organized Marxist secret societies. Mao learned how to recruit both workers and students to the cause of communism and how to organize study groups that would form the nucleus of a Chinese Communist Party.

The address where a small group of communists was established in Shanghai. *Right*: Mao Tse-Tung in 1921.

In July, Mao received the news that Zhang Jingyao, the hated Governor of Changsha, had been overthrown by a more sympathetic warlord. Mao returned to Hunan and was offered a prestigious job at his old First Normal School, as director of its primary school. The generous salary enabled him to rent a comfortable cottage, Clear Water Pool House, and at last to marry Yang Kaihui.

Mao and Yang Kuihui held meetings at their home. From the New People's Study Society they recruited members for a communist study group. Following the example set for him by Chen in Shanghai, Mao founded a Socialist Youth Corps and initiated a Cultural Book Society that made radical political writings available to the people. He also began to organize a movement to bring self-government to the citizens of Hunan and helped the craftsmen of the province to form trade unions to fight for fairer pay. Mao worked hard, growing tired and thin, but he was happy in the knowledge that he and his wife were helping their people.

Founding the Party

In May 1921, Mao Tse-tung received a summons to Shanghai for an important, top-secret meeting. At the end of the month he left Changsha, travelling under an assumed name and dressed as a tradesman. In Shanghai he was joined by eleven other young men – all of them around Mao's own age of 27. They were there to take the first big step towards revolution, to found a Communist Party of China along the lines of the one that had successfully won control in Russia.

They met for three days in the French Concession of the city, in a girls' school that was closed for the summer holiday. The Shanghai police, however, caught wind of this strange convention of young men and raided the school. All the delegates managed to escape to the lake resort of Jia Xing, outside the city, and, masquerading as holidaymakers, completed their conference on a boat floating about the lake.

The delegates at this First Congress of the Chinese Communist Party resolved to fight alone, without attempting to make any alliance with Sun Yat-sen and the Guomindang. Following Marx's teachings to the letter, they would win over the "proletariat", the industrial workers, who would, in turn, rise and overthrow the exploiters of their labour. So true to Marx were these first Chinese Communists that they failed even to think about the potential for revolution that existed among the great majority of the Chinese poor, the country's farmland peasants. Mao, surprisingly, was as guilty of this oversight as the others.

Back in Hunan, Mao Tse-tung worked hard to enlist members in the new Communist Party; among the first to join were his wife, and his brothers and sister. In October,

Stamp issued in 1949, during the early days of the People's Republic of China, to celebrate the 28th anniversary of the foundation of the Chinese Communist Party.

Sun Yat-sen with his American-educated second wife, Soong Ching-ling. Sun's first marriage, like Mao's had been an arranged one. Soong Ching-ling influenced Sun in favour of an alliance between the Guomindang and the Communists. She was later to become Vice-Chairman of the People's Republic of China.

Mikhail Borodin, the Russian adviser to the Guomindang during its alliance with the Communists, seen here in March 1927.

Mao was elected secretary of the Party in Hunan. He resolved to go directly to the workers to learn of their plight and to win them over to the Party.

Mao travelled, again in disguise, to Anyuan, a coal-mining region in southern Hunan, where he found a place to live with a poor miner's family. He went down into the pits with the miners and crawled with them along the stifling, narrow tunnels; he saw how they slaved underground for up to 15 hours a day to earn a miserable wage. Mao talked with them about their rights as workers and as human beings. By January 1922, Mao, assisted by his brother Mao Zemin, had set up a Communist Party group, or "cell", in Anyuan. He visited other towns in Hunan, and spoke with other workers; soon the party had some 12,000 members there.

An alliance

The Chinese Communist vow not to join with the Guomindang was short-lived. The young Party had the support of the Russians, and Lenin, the Russian leader, knew that Sun Yat-sen and the Guomindang had been refused military aid from the West in their fight to unite China. As a united China could be a valuable ally for Russia against the capitalist West, Lenin offered Sun the aid he needed on condition that Sun take members of the Chinese Communist Party into the Guomindang.

Lenin's agents explained their plan to the Chinese Communists. Let the middle-class Guomindang perform the dirty job of rising against the rich ruling classes, they said. The workers, the Communists, could overthrow the Guomindang later.

31

After the Communists accepted an alliance with the Guomindang in 1923, Mao was chosen by the Party to represent them on the Guomindang Executive Committee. Politics now occupied Mao's life completely. He was always on the move, organizing new cells throughout Hunan, attending Party conferences in Shanghai and Guangzhou, and working on Guomindang committees. Mao's responsibilities often conflicted, and he found himself being criticized by his fellow Communists for not being revolutionary enough and being suspected by the Guomindang for being too radical. The strain finally took its toll in early 1925. Mao fell ill from physical and mental exhaustion when he was on Party business in Shanghai. The doctors ordered him to have a complete rest.

Return to
Shaoshan

Mao's illness was a blessing in disguise. He returned to Hunan, not to the busy city of Changsha but to the farmhouse where he had grown up in Shaoshan.

For years, Mao had been living in cities. He had been surrounded by well-educated young people and by old, distinguished intellectuals. The political principles he had learned taught him to concentrate on the workers in the factories and the coal mines. Now Mao was back among his own people, the peasants, and working on the family farm. Bringing in the crops and sowing the fields, Mao

32

Mao Tse-tung in 1925.

The building in Shaoshan where Mao set up a peasant evening school, one of over twenty that he set up in Hunan in 1925. His wife, Yang Kaihui lectured here.

regained his health. During the spring of 1925, Mao visited other villages, working and talking with the ordinary people of the countryside.

Here were people whose everyday lives had been affected by the political changes in China. Their fields had been ravaged by the armies of the warlords; their meagre crops and savings had been plundered by the landlords and rent collectors. Yet instead of accepting their individual fates, peasants all over the countryside had joined together. They had wrested land from its uncaring and greedy owners. Working in groups, they had helped each other to earn a living. This, Mao realized, was something very much like communism, but practised by people who had never heard of Karl Marx.

It dawned on Mao that the peasants were the real key to a Chinese Communist revolution. With renewed vigour, Mao returned to his work, creating peasant organizations throughout Hunan. His hope, as he was to write a year and a half later, was that: "In a very short time . . . several hundred million peasants will rise like a mighty storm, like a hurricane, a force so swift and violent that no power, however great, will be able to hold it back. . . They will sweep all the imperialists, warlords, corrupt officials, local tyrants and evil gentry into their graves."

The Director of the Political Department at the Whampoa Military Academy was a future comrade of Mao at the head of the Chinese Communist party, Chou En-lai.

The funeral procession of Sun Yat-sen in July 1929, when his remains were placed in a magnificent tomb close to those of the Ming dynasty Emperors, near Nanking.

While Mao was laying the foundations for a peasant revolution, however, the Guomindang was preparing for battle. In early 1925, Sun Yat-sen travelled to Peking, to form a pact with the Manchurian warlord Zhang Zuolin against the other warlords of the north. But Sun was never able to achieve this goal. He was already gravely ill with cancer. On 12th March 1925, he died in Peking at the age of 58.

Sun's successor as leader of the Guomindang was a wealthy 37-year-old military man called Chiang Kai-shek. He had been a close aide to Sun and had been sent to Moscow to study the organization and training of the Red Army. On his return to China in 1924, Chiang was made the first commandant of the Russian-funded Whampoa Military Academy, which was intended to build a strong Guomindang army.

In 1926, Chiang launched his army on a Northern expedition to conquer China. Expertly trained Guomindang troops swept northwards from the city of Guangzhou, defeating all the warlords in their path.

Chiang's military successes had an unexpected result in the shape of a peasant uprising. The poor people of the countryside set fire to the property of the rich and to the records of the rent collectors, seized the land and redistributed it amongst themselves. The poor of the cities also took part; as Chiang's troops approached, workers went on strike and drove away their wealthy employers.

This revolt by the common people made the defeat of the warlords all the more thorough. But it worried Chiang. The workers and peasants had been educated and organized by

A busy street in Shanghai, China's main industrial city and port, in 1927.

Chiang Kai-shek, photographed around 1927.

Stamp issued in 1929 to celebrate the "unification" of China under Chiang Kai-shek.

the Communists. He could see the day when they would overwhelm the Guomindang. Chiang did not want communism in China. He wanted to transform the remains of the old feudal system into a capitalist society. In this, he had the support of wealthy Chinese and foreign businessmen, who secretly informed Chiang that he would have their financial backing if he could put down the rising Communist tide.

Chiang made his move in the spring of 1927. In March, his troops approached Shanghai. Within the city, Chiang's Communist allies roused the workers to strike, attacked the army garrison and conquered the city, which they proudly handed to their Guomindang commander. Three weeks later, without warning, Chiang ordered his troops to turn against the Communists. Thousands of unsuspecting people were cut down by Guomindang bullets.

Elsewhere in China, Chiang's orders were carried out as well. In a few months, the Guomindang Army slashed the membership of the Communist Party from almost 60,000 to 10,000. Any signs of peasant revolt were immediately quelled by Chiang's troops. Workers' unions in the cities were disbanded. All Russian military advisors were unceremoniously sent home.

In June 1928, Chiang Kai-shek took Peking. With the full approval of the West and the wealthy, he declared himself President and "Generalissimo", the most supreme general, of the Nationalist Republic of China.

Chiang's battles were, however, far from over. Hiding in the countryside, Communist rebels were gathering their strength once more. Among them, helping to harness the revolutionary power of the peasants into a well-disciplined but highly unusual fighting force, was Mao Tse-tung.

35

4. Wilderness and War

At the end of 1927, Mao Tse-tung led a unit of Communist soldiers eastwards from Changsha, which they had failed to take from the Guomindang. There were only a few hundred men left, all of them exhausted and dispirited by their hopeless fighting. In December, they arrived in Jinggangshan, at the border of the Hunan, Jiangxi and Guangdong provinces, a barren mountain region very much like the retreats of the storybook rebels Mao had read about as a boy.

Mao's retreat with his troops defied the orders of the Communist Party leaders, who believed that their soldiers should continue to attack the cities. Mao felt differently. He wanted to build a strong army of peasants, who could fight and win against the Guomindang in the countryside that they knew.

In Jinggangshan, Mao joined forces with two bandit chieftains who were willing to lend their power to Mao and the Red Army so long as they could do battle with the Guomindang. Later, in May, Mao's forces were joined by those of Zhu De and Lin Biao, two Communist commanders who had experienced the same humiliating defeats as Mao and were equally eager to build a better Red Army.

Mao Tse-tung (third from the left) with the other leaders of his unsuccessful offensive in 1927, which is known as the Autumn Harvest Uprising.

36

Mao Tse-tung in 1927.

One advantage seldom held by any army, especially the ruthless troops of the Guomindang, was the support of the local people, whose lives were turned upside down by the presence of thousands of soldiers. Mao, Zhu and Lin set out to win over the village people of Jinggangshan by enforcing a simple but very strict set of regulations for the Red Army.

The soldiers were to obey all orders. They were not to confiscate anything belonging to the local people. If they borrowed something, they were to return it as soon as possible; if they damaged anything, they were to replace it immediately. They had to be honest at all times and to pay for anything they needed. Personal cleanliness was a necessity. Most important, the soldiers were ordered to show the highest courtesy and politeness to the people, especially to women, and to offer them help whenever they could.

These rules gained Mao's soldiers the support of the peasantry. But Mao and the other commanders were even more strict in preparing their troops for the fighting that was to come. They adopted four short rhyming slogans, which each took only four characters to write in Chinese and were easily memorized but contained all the battle tactics a Red Army soldier would need. No doubt the eloquent Mao composed them himself:

1. When the enemy advances, we retreat!
2. When the enemy halts and encamps, we trouble them!
3. When the enemy seeks to avoid a battle, we attack!
4. When the enemy retreats, we pursue!

These are the basic principles of guerrilla warfare, with which a small but perfectly disciplined and mobile group of men can defeat superior, well-organized forces through cunning and speed, hitting when their opponents are weak or off their guard, and disappearing into the countryside when challenged. Although Chiang continually sent battalions to flush out the rebels in Jinggangshan, Mao's carefully drilled troops unfailingly drove off the Guomindang forces.

Mao's Red Army was confidently in control of the province of Jiangxi. They declared their base to be a "soviet", an independent state governed by its own people's council, like the soviets set up by the Russian Communists. But rather than allow Mao and the other generals of the Red Army to increase their strength in the relative safety of rural Jiangxi, the Central Committee of the Chinese Communist Party felt that its armies should be getting on with the business of bringing about a workers' revolution in the cities. In mid-1930, Mao was ordered to attack Changsha.

37

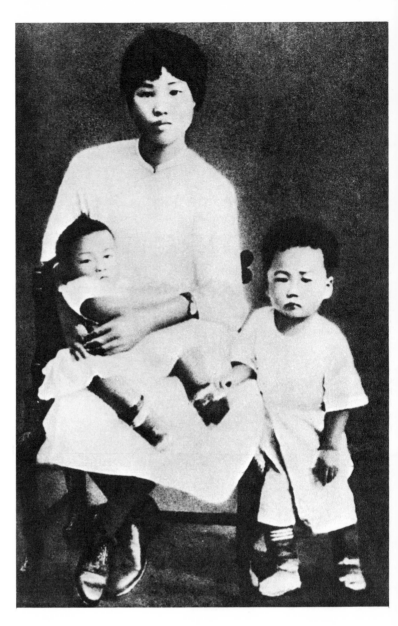

Mao's wife, Yang Kaihui, and their two sons, Mao Anying and Mao Anqing. She was executed by the Guomindang in November 1930.

Changsha was still a stronghold of underground Communist activity. This was partly led by Mao's wife, Yang Kaihui, who had stayed behind at Clear Water Pool House to care for their two young sons. Mao himself was well-known throughout Hunan as a Communist leader. Indeed, the Guomindang made it known there that a large reward would be paid for his capture, dead or alive.

Chiang Kai-shek, who could not afford to lose Changsha and the rest of Hunan, poured his best troops into the province. Mao and the Red Army met heavy resistance when they attacked Changsha. Thousands of Communist soldiers were killed, as Mao's men stormed the city walls again and again. After 13 days of hopeless battle, Mao defied his orders to take Changsha at all costs and led the survivors of his Red Army battalions back to Jiangxi.

Terrible as this defeat was, Mao suffered an even greater personal tragedy. During the siege of Changsha, the warlord governor of the city took Mao's wife, his two sons, his sister and the wives of his brothers as prisoners. He brutally questioned the women for information on Mao's activities; they told him nothing. Finally, he released Mao's sons and his sisters-in-law. Mao's wife and sister were beheaded.

The Jiangxi Soviet

Mao's two brothers, Mao Zetan (*below*) and Mao Zemin (*right*). Like Yang Kaihui, they joined the Communist Party in 1921 and were active in it. Both were captured and executed by the Guomindang, Mao Zetan in 1935 and Mao Zemin some ten years later.

With the military losses of the Red Army behind them, the members of the Jiangxi Soviet gradually improved their lives under their new social system. Taxes were drastically cut, and the land was shared out among the people. Schools were established, and unemployment disappeared, as did the more tragic social evils such as drug addiction, child slavery and prostitution.

But Chiang Kai-shek's attacks on Jiangxi went on. From December 1930 to October 1933, Chiang sent some 850,000 Guomindang soldiers in four military campaigns to exterminate the Red Army. Each time, the Red Army was

Mao addressing a conference in Jiangxi in 1933.

able to fight off the Guomindang troops. Mao later recounted that reports had come back to him of Chiang's field commander complaining that "fighting the Reds was a 'life-time job'."

At the end of 1933, Chiang changed his tactics. He sent almost a million of his finest soldiers marching to Jiangxi, this time not to engage in major battles with the Red Army, but to surround the Jiangxi Soviet, to set up fortifications and a blockade. By cutting off Jiangxi completely, Chiang hoped to weaken it and eventually close in so that he could take it over.

In one year almost a million people in Jiangxi died from starvation and from Guomindang bombing raids and land assaults. Mao Tse-tung and other Jiangxi leaders finally decided that the only way the Red Army could survive was suddenly, unexpectedly, to leave Jiangxi for northern China, far from the southern base of the Guomindang.

The Long March

On 16th October 1934, the Red Army set out from Jiangxi on a trek that was to last over a year, a heroic episode in its history that would come to be known as "The Long March." Nobody knows exactly how far they went, but they probably covered at least 10,000 km (6,000 miles). At the start of the march there were 90,000 soldiers, joined by thousands of Jiangxi peasants, including women, children and old people, carrying whatever possessions they could on their own backs and those of their work animals. Mao Tse-tung called it a great "house removal operation".

Mao himself carried everything he owned. It amounted to very little: some books, two blankets, a sweater, an overcoat, his eating bowl and a broken umbrella. He also had a horse, a prize he had taken from a Guomindang officer, which he loaded with supplies. Mao went alongside it on foot, like his men.

They travelled by night. During the day they kept low and rested. On the fourth night, they stormed the southwestern lines of Chiang's troops. In the fight to take the Guomindang fortifications and allow the long lines of marchers to pass safely through the blockade, 25,000 Red Army soldiers died.

Every day, while the marchers rested, Guomindang aircraft swarmed overhead, strafing them with bullets. Soon Mao changed their schedule to alternating four-hour periods of walking and resting, to increase the aircrafts' difficulty in pinning them down.

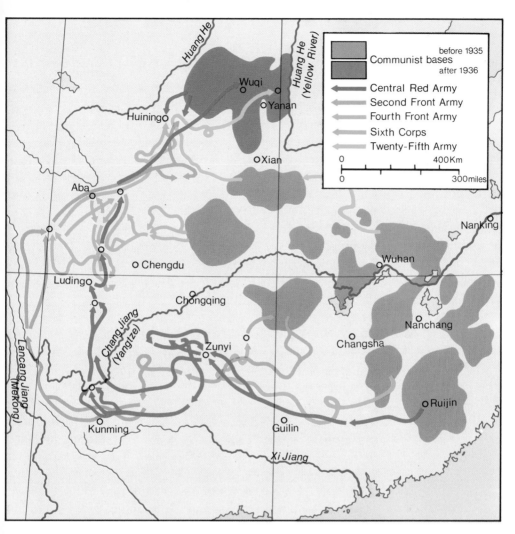

The legend on the map reads:

Communist bases — before 1935
Communist bases — after 1936
Central Red Army
Second Front Army
Fourth Front Army
Sixth Corps
Twenty-Fifth Army

0   400 Km
0   300 miles

The route of the Long March from Jiangxi Province to Shaanxi in the north of China.

At the Xiang River in Hunan, the Red Army came up against a huge Guomindang battalion. The courageous soldiers waded across the river, using their bodies to shield the unarmed peasants as they crossed. It took seven days of fighting at the river for the Red Army to drive off the Guomindang; 30,000 communist soldiers died. Mao, when he was not fighting, helped tend the wounded; he even gave away his overcoat to shield a dying soldier from the cold.

The Red Army moved westwards, fighting almost daily with Guomindang forces. In just a month and a half of marching, more than two-thirds of them had been killed. If they were to reach their destination, they would have to decide on some definite strategy for survival.

The strategy came from Mao Tse-tung. Instead of heading straight for the north, as the other leaders wished, Mao

Mao with Zhu De, who was commander-in-chief of the Red Army on the Long March.

argued for continuing to the west, to Guizhou Province, where the Guomindang forces were weak, and the Red Army would have a chance to gather its strength. Mao also made the soldiers throw away all but the barest necessities to lighten their loads. The Red Army would need to move fast. Their first success, though small, came soon: the Red Army easily defeated warlord forces in Guizhou. Afterwards, the soldiers quickly came to see Mao as their only leader.

In early January, the marchers took the city of Zunyi in northern Guizhou. At the spacious house of a warlord, the leaders of the Chinese Communist Party met to discuss their plans. Mao, they knew, had continually resisted the ill-judged plans of his superiors in the Party and had been single-handedly responsible for the victorious campaigns in Guizhou. Because the other Party officials realized that Mao was their best hope for success, they now elected him Chairman – the leader of the Party.

Mao's leadership fired the Red Army with courage, heroism and cunning. For four months, they marched in south-western China, continually changing direction to confuse and outwit Guomindang forces. Through the mountains of Yunnan Province they moved towards Sichuan and the great Yangtze River. Although Chiang had the river guarded, some of Mao's men disguised themselves as Guomindang soldiers and managed to commandeer boats; the entire army was ferried across safely.

The Dadu River, further north, was more closely guarded. Mao knew that his men were afraid. As they drew closer to the Dadu, he made every effort to rally their spirits. Marching among them, he told jokes, made up stories and composed poems that they could sing to familiar tunes.

At the town of An Renchang, they managed to capture a single boat. This could carry a small detachment across the Dadu, but it would take many days before the whole army would be safely on the other side. By then, Chiang's men would have had time to surround them.

So Mao led the bulk of the Red Army westward, towards the nearest bridge across the Dadu River, the Luding Bridge, 145 km (90 miles) away. For three nights, the soldiers ran along a narrow trail that rose high through mountain forests and then dropped down through waist-deep streams.

Luding Bridge was made of iron chains set into the sides of a rocky gorge 60 metres (200 feet) above the Dadu. Across the chains were planks, over which traffic could cross. But when Mao's soldiers reached the bridge, they found that all the planks on their side had been removed, and that the northern side of the bridge was guarded by a battery of Guomindang machine guns.

A Chinese painting of the taking of the Luding Bridge on the Dadu River.

Twenty-two Red Army soldiers volunteered to cross the bridge. They strapped guns and hand grenades to their backs and, hanging from the chains, moved across the bridge hand-over-hand. Seventeen of them were shot and plunged to their deaths; other volunteers replaced them. Finally, some came close enough to throw grenades at the gun emplacement. The Guomindang soldiers responded by setting fire to the bridge planks on their side, but Mao's soldiers rushed through the flames. Within two hours, the bridge was taken. The Red Army soldiers borrowed doors from the nearby town and laid them across the chains so the rest of the troops could cross.

The Red Army continued north through snowcapped mountains. To ward off the extreme cold, Mao made everyone drink chilli peppers and ginger boiled in water. In eastern

Crossing the mountains, the marchers climbed to well over 3,000 metres (10,000 feet).

A Chinese painting of the Red Army pushing on through the dangerously swampy grasslands of northern Sichuan Province.

Tibet, they encountered local tribes who hated the Chinese; one, the Manzi, had a queen who threatened to boil alive any of her subjects who helped the Red Army. For the first time, Mao's men had to fight for their food. Mao sadly remarked at the time that "to buy one sheep costs the life of one man."

North of the mountains, they came to the great grasslands of China, a region where rain falls almost non-stop. Hundreds of soldiers stumbled and fell into the swamps that surrounded them; their comrades were helpless to come to their aid. By the time they left the grasslands, only 7,000 soldiers remained.

On 20th October 1935, these survivors reached the northern province of Shaanxi, where Communist armies from elsewhere in China had joined together to form a safe base. Chairman Mao and his soldiers had travelled for 368 days. They had passed through 18 mountain ranges and crossed 24 rivers. They had marched across 12 different provinces and met six different native tribes. Besides the continual threat of the Guomindang, they had also fought against 12 warlord armies and taken 62 towns and cities. Almost all along the way, they had won friends and supporters for the Red Army among the common people.

45

5. Turmoil and Triumph

Mao Tse-tung and his followers settled in the tiny village of Baoan, nestled among the hills of Shaanxi Province, on the edge of the great Gobi Desert. In this desolate, sandy region they slowly began to recuperate from the hardships they had suffered both as individuals and as a political movement.

Mao, now 42 years old, was extremely thin, which made him look even taller than his six-foot height. His hair was long and shaggy. His clothes were worn out and patched. But he had his health and his hopes for rebuilding the Communist forces.

The Communists occupied a series of caves in the hillsides surrounded by date palms and walnut trees. Mao put his men to work with the local peasants and enforced the same strict code of behaviour for them as he had laid down in Jiangxi. Working on the land built up the health of the Red Army soldiers; it also won them the friendship of the people of Shaanxi.

Mao led a quiet, solitary life; his third wife, He Zizhen, who had been with him on the Long March, left for Moscow to receive medical treatment for shrapnel wounds (she did not return and was divorced from Mao in 1937). Mao worked all night in his cave, writing and making plans. During the day he slept, went for walks to meet the local people and gardened in a tiny patch below the cave where he raised tomatoes and rough tobacco for smoking. He also continued to write poetry.

Mao early in 1938 at the Kangda Cave University in Yanan, and addressing a session of the Sixth Central Committee of the Chinese Communist Party at Yanan in November 1938.

A mass meeting in Yanan, early in 1938.

46

Communist soldiers on the road in Shaanxi Province in 1937.

In late 1936, the town of Yanan in Shaanxi Province became the new capital of the Chinese Soviet Republic. Land was taken from the landlords and redistributed among the people, rents and taxes were cut, food was evenly shared out, and a basic education, both in reading and writing and in communism, was offered to everyone. For the moment, the Communists of Shaanxi were safe.

Other dangers now began to worry Mao, dangers that threatened not only the Communist Party and himself, but the whole of China. In 1931, the Japanese had invaded the northeastern province of Manchuria, a major industrial area; since then, they had gradually been spreading their influence

Chiang Kai-shek and his wife, Soong Mei-ling. She was the sister of Sun Yat-sen's wife, Soong Ching-ling, who supported the Communists against the Guomindang.

Zhang Xueliang (in uniform) with his captive, Chiang Kai-shek (in long cloak). *Right*: a refugee carrying his children. With the Guomindang fighting the Communists and the Japanese invading, many Chinese were forced to leave their homes in the 1930s.

to the south and west. Chiang Kai-shek, however, had done nothing to stop them, as he was still blindly preoccupied with the Communists.

In December 1936, Chiang flew to the city of Xian in southern Shaanxi to plan a new anti-Communist military campaign. But on his first night in Xian, Chiang was kidnapped by the Manchurian commander, Zhang Xueliang, and his troops, who wanted the Generalissimo to recapture their homeland from the Japanese. If he refused to help them, he would die.

In Yanan, Mao received word that Chiang was being held prisoner. Five months earlier, Mao had personally appealed to Chiang in a telegram, asking him to join together to fight the Japanese and quoting an old Chinese maxim, "Brothers quarrelling at home will join forces against attacks from the outside." Although his plea had been ignored, Mao now saw his chance to persuade Chiang to form a united front against Japan. Mao sent his second-in-command, the able Chou En-lai, to Xian to negotiate for Chiang's release.

Following Mao's instructions, Chou reached an agreement with Chiang Kai-shek that secured the Guomindang leader's safety. Mao cared more about China's security than about his own or his Party's. He agreed to disband the

Chinese Soviet Republic in exchange for Chiang's cancellation of his anti-Communist campaign. The Red Army would be renamed the Eighth Route Army, and it would become a division under the overall command of Chiang in the forthcoming fight with Japan.

Fighting the Japanese

The united Chinese forces did not have long to wait. Japanese troops fought a bloody skirmish with Guomindang troops on 8th July 1937 at the Marco Polo Bridge near Peking. War had begun.

Things did not go well for the Guomindang. Although they fought valiantly, they were overwhelmed by superior Japanese strength. One by one, Peking, Shanghai, Nanking, Hankou and Guangzhou fell. Chiang Kai-shek had to flee to remote Chongqing in central China.

The Japanese also overran the Communist territory in northwestern China. Under Mao's guidance, though, the Eighth Route Army waged a perfect guerrilla war. The Japanese occupied the major cities and controlled the railway lines, rivers and roads, but Mao's men never met them in conventional battle. Instead, they attacked at night, from behind; when the Japanese challenged them, they vanished among the population. "The people," Mao wrote, "are the sea; and the army are the fishes swimming in that sea."

To destroy the Communists, the Japanese initiated a campaign in Shaanxi and neighbouring provinces called, with brutal directness, the "Three Alls": "Loot all, burn all, kill all." Wherever Communist influence was suspected, the invaders laid waste the countryside. But still Mao's Eighth

The Japanese arrive: a senior officer of the Japanese naval landing party drives through Shanghai in October 1936. Following his staff car is a truckload of Japanese marines.

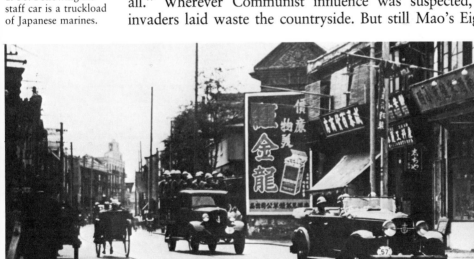

Route Army continued to sabotage the morale of the Japanese, and, through their courage, to win the hearts of the peasantry.

1939 marked the beginning of World War II, with Japan's allies, Germany and Italy, attempting to conquer their own neighbours. The allies were too involved in the European war to be greatly concerned with China. Then, on 7th December 1941, the United States was plunged into the World War when its naval base at Pearl Harbor in Hawaii was bombarded in a surprise Japanese air attack. Now China had an ally. While the Americans fought the Japanese on the Pacific Ocean, they also supplied the Chinese with weapons to combat the enemy on land.

Chiang Kai-shek, as the acknowledged leader of China and therefore the recipient of this aid, had other plans for his American supplies. The popular success of the Eighth Route Army increased Chiang's hatred of the Communists. From the safety of Chongqing he watched Mao's forces battle with the Japanese, all the while hoarding his American equipment for an eventual war against the Communists.

The war with Japan ended in August 1945, when the United States demolished the cities of Hiroshima and Nagasaki with atom bombs. The end of the war left the way open for the final round of the life-and-death struggle between the Guomindang and the Communists. As in the past, there was first a brief attempt to patch up the differences between the two sides.

On 28th August 1945, the 52-year-old Mao Tse-tung waved goodbye to the crowds in Yanan and Mao boarded an aircraft for Chongqing, where he was to meet Chiang Kai-shek in an attempt to form a government of national unity that would rebuild China.

Stamp issued in 1945 to commemorate the inauguration of Chiang Kai-shek as President of the Republic of China.

Mao with Chou En-Lai in Yanan in 1945, and arriving in Chongqing on 28th August 1945 with the American Ambassador, Patrick J. Hurley.

50

Mao Tse-tung and Chiang Kai-shek drink to the success of their negotiations in Chongqing.

Mao was still willing to compromise with Chiang. He arrived at Chongqing with a quiet, respectful air that was not altered by the wildly enthusiastic reception given to him by the people of the city. But the stiff-backed, polished leader of the Guomindang felt only contempt for the modest peasant from Hunan: in their private meetings Chiang did not conceal his feelings. After 45 days of conferences, the two men reached an uneasy agreement to form a democratic government and to merge their armies. Neither man, in his heart, believed the agreement could last for long.

Defeating the Guomindang

Both sides started to arm themselves for the inevitable fight. Mao wrote in 1945, "We take up swords, too, following his example . . . As Chiang Kai-shek is now sharpening his swords, we must sharpen ours too."

Chiang's "swords" finally descended on the Communists in July 1946. A squadron of American-built bombers swooped over the hillsides of Yanan, attacking Communist headquarters in the first step of Chiang's final campaign to annihilate his sworn enemies.

On the face of it, Chiang certainly had the advantage; he had a hundred American military advisors and more than a thousand million dollars of American aid. What he did not have, though, was the military cunning that Mao had acquired in over 15 years of defensive fighting.

Mao fooled Chiang into thinking that the Guomindang were winning. He allowed them to pierce deep into Communist territory. As Chiang's crack troops approached a Communist-held city, town or village, Mao's men fled. Chiang was sure victory was near; but Mao knew who was really winning.

51

Mao leading the People's Liberation Army in its campaign in northwestern China in 1947. This photograph published in a Chinese book of the late 1970s has not just been coloured. It has also been retouched to remove a second figure on horseback behind the soldier in the straw hat. In earlier books, this figure is said to be Mao's wife, Jiang Qing, who went with him on campaign. *Right*: Communist infantry storm the walls of Jin Xian in Liaoning Province in 1946.

The more territory Chiang took, the more spread out his troops were. Guomindang forces were wasted in taking and securing towns and districts that the Communists had no need to hold. The Red Army, now renamed the People's Liberation Army, sang a song that summed up their strategy:

Keep men, lose land. Land can be taken again.

Keep land, lose men. Land and men both lost.

Mao and his soldiers kept constantly on the move, always changing direction, just as they had during the Long March. This time their movements were confined to Shaanxi, and their purpose was not simply self-preservation but to exhaust and defeat the pursuing Guomindang.

Their route twisted and turned northwards from Yanan. They stopped in small villages sympathetic with their cause, but never told the people who their illustrious guest was. Mao, for his own safety and that of his peasant hosts, used a pseudonym. As comrade Li Desheng, Chairman Mao was just a member of the People's Liberation Army – an important one, but never expecting any special treatment.

He insisted on eating the same simple food that the villagers ate. His diet consisted of a coarse millet gruel and elm leaves. Mao lost weight, but he laughed it away, saying that he could march better if he was thinner.

As was his habit, Mao worked at night, sitting beside an oil lamp and planning the strategy for his own group and for Communist battalions elsewhere in China. Couriers arrived bringing news, and Mao also kept up with developments by way of a battery radio.

He used his spare time for education. Every evening he studied foreign languages, and he always carried a book in his pocket so that he could read a page or two during the odd free moment. He encouraged his soldiers to do likewise. Mao, as much a teacher as a leader, discussed with the men the books they read.

"An army without culture," Mao wrote, "is a dull-witted army, and a dull-witted army cannot defeat the enemy." A habit, established in Yanan, of presenting poetry readings, concerts and plays was continued at every opportunity. Of course, every event served a political end, carrying the message of communism to its audience.

Mao was helped in planning cultural activities by his fourth wife, Jiang Qing. She had been an actress in the film industry of Shanghai, using the name Lan Ping – "Blue Apple". In 1933, at the age of 21, she joined the Communist Youth League there; five years later, she moved to Yanan, where she trained Communist theatrical groups and, through her work, met Mao. They married in 1939 and had two daughters.

The People's Liberation Army continued on the move, but never left a village without showing gratitude to the people. Any buildings they had used were carefully swept clean. Each soldier was required to return or replace anything he had borrowed or broken. Each family was personally visited by the soldiers, who said goodbye and offered thanks for the hospitality.

Such sincerity was as effective in winning popular support for the People's Liberation Army as Mao's tactics were in winning battles. By 1948, the Communists' ranks were swollen with new recruits, including defectors from the Guomindang. Mao's army now used captured American equipment. Gradually it swept across China, taking the offensive and capturing cities, which, Mao remarked, "fell like ripe fruit." Chiang Kai-shek and his remaining followers departed to set up a government on the island of Formosa (now called Taiwan), 150 km (90 miles) from the Chinese coast.

Mao Tse-tung proclaims the foundation of the People's Republic of China on 1st October 1949.

On 1st October 1949, Mao Tse-tung stood before hundreds of thousands of jubilant Chinese people in Tian An Men Square in Peking, on the balcony of a palace that had once been occupied by the Emperors, the Sons of Heaven. Mao was dressed as most of the people were, in simple country clothes and a cloth cap. As Chairman of the victorious Communist Party, he proclaimed the foundation of the People's Republic of China, with bold, stirring words: "The Chinese people will never again be humiliated! We have stood up! Let the world tremble!"

53

6. Mao's China

With the founding of the People's Republic of China in October 1949, the life story of Mao Tse-tung became inseparable from the history of his country. His dedication to China had caused him to live in constant hardship, endangering the lives of those he cared about and putting his own life at risk countless times for the sake of building a new nation. Mao had gradually come to stop thinking of himself simply as "I". He always expressed himself as "we " to indicate that he and his fellow Communists had common beliefs about helping the people of China.

That is not to say that every thought Mao had was correct, that every idea was accepted by the Communist Party, or that every decision he made was the right one. Nor was Mao constantly in control of China. But he always worked for what he felt was the good of his country; his thoughts became the thoughts of his people, his devotion their inspiration. The Chinese came to give Mao nicknames to express the roles he played in modern China: "The Great Helmsman", "The Great Leader" or "The Great Teacher". Mao always preferred the last title, and he was the people's guiding light as they learned to shake off thousands of years of repression.

Russia and Korea

Two months after he had led his party to power, Mao Tse-tung left China for the first time. He travelled to Moscow, for a meeting with the Russian leader Joseph Stalin.

The new Chinese nation had been badly hurt by years of war. Its industries and farms were in ruins. Under Chiang Kai-shek its economy had collapsed. Between 1946 and 1948, prices in the country had doubled 67 times, and in the last six months of Chiang Kai Shek's leadership they had risen by 85,000 times. Worse still, Chiang had taken China's gold reserves with him when he fled to Taiwan. The People's Republic of China, under Mao, had the manpower and the unity to remedy the situation, but it needed outside advice and financial help. Russia, the oldest and largest Communist country, was the logical choice.

Stalin, however, was suspicious of Mao. The Soviet leader was a strong, hard man who ruled ruthlessly by fear. But Mao arrived proud and unfearing, asking for help and expecting to receive it as China's rightful due from a fellow Communist state. Stalin had to be sure that once China had

In the last years of Guomindang rule in China, the currency collapsed. Even a postage stamp like this one could cost five million dollars.

Mao Tse-tung in Russia, with Russian leaders Bulganin (centre) and Stalin.

recovered and rebuilt itself, it would not turn its back on the world Communist revolution or forget the debt of gratitude it owed to Russia.

Mao left Moscow after two months of exhausting negotiations. As well as Russian recognition of his government's right to rule the Chinese nation, he returned home with 300 million dollars worth of credit for Soviet industrial supplies and advisers. Before he could even begin to use this assistance, Mao had the chance to show Stalin how committed the Chinese were to communism.

During World War II, the tiny country of Korea, a peninsula near China's northeastern border with the Soviet Union, was occupied by the Japanese. After the war, the Russians were given control of the northern half of the country, the Americans the south, and Korea became a battleground between communism and capitalism. In 1950, after countless skirmishes, the North Korean forces swept southwards.

Rather than just driving the North Koreans back to their side of the border, the Americans and South Koreans under General Douglas MacArthur pursued them towards the Yalu River, the border of the Chinese province of Manchuria. Mao Tse-tung had no choice but to join the battle. In late 1950 he sent the People's Liberation Army to the defence of both the North Koreans and of China.

Fighting raged for three years. In the end, an uneasy truce was called, with the border between North and South Korea unchanged from what it had been before the fighting. Russia had shouldered none of the burden of the war, and almost one million Chinese soldiers had been killed or wounded. Among the dead was one of Mao's sons, Mao Anying, the commander of an infantry division.

Mao's son, Mao Anying.

"The outstanding thing about China's 600 million people," Mao once wrote, "is that they are 'poor and blank'. This may seem a bad thing, but in reality it is a good thing. Poverty gives rise to the desire for change, the desire for action and the desire for revolution. On a blank sheet of paper free from any mark, the freshest and most beautiful characters can be written, the freshest and most beautiful pictures can be painted."

In the early 1950s, with the help of Russian aid, with the secure knowledge that he could defend his country's borders, and with the support of his Party and the vast majority of his poverty-stricken people, Mao began to write the characters, to paint the picture, of the new China.

One important goal was to rescue the economy. The new government took over all aspects of trade in China: the heavy industries, big businesses and banks. A new State Bank tightly controlled the flow of money. Prices of goods were fixed, and inflation, the rise of prices, was halted.

In the countryside, Mao imposed the programme of "land reform" that he had previously applied in the provinces where he and his men had sought refuge from the Guomindang. The land was taken, by force if necessary, from the wealthy landlords and distributed among the peasants who worked it. Equal shares for equal work went to women, as Mao had always believed in their equality with men.

Land reform, Mao realized, would not solve China's problems completely unless ways of thinking were also changed. He began a programme of "thought reform" to educate the Chinese people. Meetings, rallies, plays and concerts introduced the people to Marxist thought. Street posters, newspapers, books and every radio broadcast spread the message of communism in a massive propaganda campaign.

Reviewing the Peking May Day parade of 1951. Left to right: Vice-Chairmen Liu Shaoqi and Zhu De, Chairman Mao Tsetung and Premier Chou En-lai.

A parade in Peking, a Chinese illustration published in 1951.

Stamp issued in 1950 to commemorate the first anniversary of the founding of the People's Republic of China, showing Mao, the country's flag and a parade.

Thought reform had its harsher aspects as well. This was, after all, the revolution Mao had worked towards, and he had long ago observed that, "A revolution is not a dinner party ... A revolution is an insurrection by which one class overthrows another." He also said: "Whoever wants to oppose communism must prepare to be smashed to pieces."

The rich, the landlords and the Guomindang supporters, indeed all those who opposed communism, were put on trial. Sometimes they were sentenced to *si-xiang gai-zao*, the so-called "brainwashing": they were sent to labour camps where they were subjected to harsh, occasionally brutal work, unending criticism of their past errors and continual bombardment with Marxist philosophy, until they were considered "re-educated".

Many others, however, were not so fortunate. They were considered irredeemably guilty. Death was their sentence. Estimates of the number of offenders put to death during the early years of the People's Republic vary from 150,000 to more than a million. Countless others, no doubt, lost their lives in the "re-education camps".

The large majority of the Chinese people, however, accepted and endorsed Mao's viewpoint. In 1954, China had moved a step closer to true communism: villagers all over the country began to pool their individual landholdings, forming "co-operatives" that they farmed as a group with jointly owned machinery and animals, and jointly shared profits. They found this made their work easier, their harvests more bountiful and their earnings greater.

This scheme formed part of Mao's First Five Year plan, begun in 1953. The plan succeeded. China's grain harvest

"Ready to submit a production report to Mao Tse-tung", a Chinese illustration published in 1951.

reached a staggering 182 million tons in 1956, more than two-thirds greater than the 1949 harvest. Even more progress was made in industry; with Russian help, China produced about three million tons of steel in 1956, almost nine times more than in 1950.

A hundred flowers

In 1956, Mao Tse-tung was already looking beyond his First Five Year Plan to the future. Certainly the Russians had helped China to rebuild itself, but the emphasis had been on heavy industry and on strict government control over planning. Mao, on the other hand, wanted to pay more attention to rural China and to allow the people some local control over their daily lives. He could also see the possibility of Russian assistance turning into Russian domination, as it had in Eastern Europe. Mao knew he had to reduce China's dependence on Russia.

Not everyone in the Chinese Communist Party agreed with Mao. He would indeed be swimming against a tide of contrary opinion if he moved away from the Russian model of communism. As if to illustrate this, and to demonstrate his power to overcome all obstacles, Mao publicly swam across the Yangtze River at the city of Wuhan, where the water was more than a mile across and the current swift, and he wrote a poem to express his philosophy both as a swimmer and as a politician.

The year 1956 closed with Mao's call to the Chinese people to "let a hundred flowers bloom, a hundred schools of thought contend." He wanted the people of China, particularly its scholars, to speak out and express their views, even to the point of criticizing their leaders. His hope was that, though these "hundred schools of thought" might contend, they would all support the basic beliefs of Marxism and offer constructive criticism to strengthen China's Communist ideals.

Mao was wrong. His call to China was answered with a torrent of abuse against its rulers and against communism that rocked both the Communist Party of China and Mao himself. He met this problem in the way he had dealt with so many others during his life. He thought deeply about it, reasoning through all aspects of the failure of his "Hundred Flowers" movements. Then he wrote down his ideas in a simple but thoroughly scholarly essay.

He stated his belief that the Chinese people should, above all, be free to make their own non-political decisions and that, for example, it would be harmful for the state to insist on one particular style of art or school of thought and to ban the others. What would not be tolerated was criticism of socialism, communism or Marxism. Questions of political belief could be resolved only by "drawing a clear distinction between ourselves and the enemy." Anyone who criticized the political foundations of China would now be considered an enemy of the Chinese state.

The Great Leap Forward

Mao next turned to the problems presented by five years of Russian aid and the need for greater Chinese independence. His first move was to strengthen the hold of communism in rural China.

At the end of the first Five Year Plan, Mao inspects the first car to be made in China, the East Wind, on its arrival from the factory in Manchuria in June 1958.

One of a series of stamps issued in 1957 to celebrate the virtues of co-operative agriculture.

Mao among millet crops during a tour of the Honan countryside in 1958.

In 1958, the Communist Party began to organize already existing co-operative farms, in which the land was individually owned but collectively worked, into large communes. The communes roughly followed the borders of the old Chinese counties or districts. The average size of communes was about 25,000 people, but some included as many as 50,000 in a hundred small villages. The land was owned by the commune as a whole. Each commune, it was hoped, would become self-sufficient, with its own schools, its own health facilities and its own local government.

The commune movement was imposed throughout China, and as part of his new emphasis on rural China, Mao also initiated plans for bringing industry to the communes. If the vast manpower of China could be put to work in its spare time producing iron and steel in small, back garden furnaces, the country could make great economic advances without the help of Russia.

Mao named his programme "The Great Leap Forward." In some ways it was. China found it could do without Russian assistance. The Chinese people received valuable training in industrial methods along with their growing knowledge of advanced farming techniques. They were also largely allowed to govern themselves on a local level.

However, during the Great Leap Forward the Chinese nation also took a giant step backwards. The years 1959–61 saw a series of calamitous droughts and floods throughout China. The newly organized communes, having changed over too quickly from their old methods, were not prepared to deal with the disasters. In 1961, China had to buy ten million tons of grain from abroad to prevent a famine.

The maize harvest on a commune.

60

Mao Tse-tung and Liu
Shaoqi after the
election of Liu as
Chairman of the
People's Republic of
China.

Mao's gradual easing of dependence on Russia was accompanied by severe Russian criticism of Mao's new policies. In 1960, Stalin's successor, Nikita Khrushchev, suddenly withdrew all Soviet aid and technicians from China, leaving industrial projects ranging from factories to hydroelectric dams half-finished.

Mao appeared to have failed in his plans. He was forced to withdraw from the position of Chairman of the People's Republic of China, although he retained his post as Communist Party Chairman. It was in this job, barred from the practical duties of planning and governing but still in charge of the body that shaped Chinese political thought, that Mao was able to engineer his next rise to power.

The Cultural Revolution

The new Chinese head of state, Liu Shaoqi, believed in the Russian way of communism: rule by an elite group of trained experts with widespread control over the country's activities. Liu got on with the task of completing China's unfinished Russian-aided projects. While Liu ruled, Mao virtually disappeared from the public eye; rumours even spread that he had died.

But Mao was actually increasing his influence in other spheres. Lin Biao, who had been a commander in the Red Army and People's Liberation Army during the long wars against the Guomindang and the Japanese, was made Minister of Defence under Liu. A supporter of Mao's ideas, Lin Biao was responsible for compiling a small, red-bound book of extracts from Mao Tse-tung's writings. *Quotations from Chairman Mao Tse-tung*, more widely known to us simply as "The Little Red Book", became the unofficial training manual of the People's Liberation Army; every soldier was

The words of Lin Biao in his own handwriting, reproduced at the front of *Quotations from Chairman Mao Tse-tung*. "Study Chairman Mao's writings, follow his teachings and act according to his instructions."

Mao and Lin Biao shown together on a 1967 stamp.

Mao on his second swim in the Yangtze.

drilled to be a total believer in the wisdom of Mao Tse-tung. As Mao himself had observed, "Whoever wants to seize and retain state power must have a strong army." Put more bluntly in another famous quotation from the Chairman, "Every Communist must grasp the truth, 'Political power grows out of the barrel of a gun.' "

Mao also began to build another broad base of support. In 1962, he introduced a movement he called "Socialist Education". Its purpose was to instil radical Communist ideas into the young people of China. None of the staid Russian-style communists who were Mao's opponents could oppose such idealistic lessons; they did not feel that there was any real threat in Mao's programme. Yet the effect of Socialist Education was to convert the youth of China gradually to Mao's way of thinking. As Mao had observed in yet another of the *Quotations*, "The young people are the most active and vital force in society."

The truth of this statement was proved in 1966, when the conflict between factions led by Liu Shaoqi and by Mao and Lin Biao burst into the open. The incident that caused this to happen was a play performed in Peking.

The play was written by Wuhan, Deputy Mayor of the city and a backer of Chairman Liu. It told of a loyal servant to one of the Ming emperors who was dismissed without reason by his master. Mao and Lin took the play to be an attack on Mao himself, as, before his own fall from State office, he had dismissed the followers of the line later taken up by Liu Shaoqi; the play implied, then, that Mao wanted nothing more than to be an all-powerful emperor.

Wu's play was immediately attacked in the newspaper over which Mao still had control, *People's Daily*, the voice of the Chinese Communist Party, and then in *Liberation Daily*, the newspaper of Lin Biao's army. Other papers throughout China echoed Mao's displeasure, and Mao's wife, Jiang Qing, began sharply and openly to criticize this "decline" of the arts in China.

In July 1966, Mao showed China that he was fit and ready for another political fight by repeating his swim, of ten years before across the Yangtze. The 71-year-old Chairman swam in the currents for an hour. Some ten thousand swimmers joined him, and thousands of others on boats and on the shore cheered, "Chairman Mao! Chairman Mao!"

Into the battle Mao now brought the young people of China, the students whose minds he had won with the Socialist Education movement. He called to them to join in

a "Cultural Revolution", their equivalent of the revolution Mao and his peers had led in the past. They were, Mao instructed, to criticize and change everything they judged to be old, old ideas, old culture, old habits and customs, and to weed out from every level of Chinese society the "revisionists", the Soviet-style elitists who dug in their heels at the thought of revolutionary progress.

Mao's Cultural Revolution succeeded far too well. The students organized themselves into a well-disciplined junior army, the Red Guard. Waving their copies of the Little Red Book, they marched and demonstrated throughout the country. Teachers were driven from classrooms, schools were closed down, and buildings were plastered with banners bearing new revolutionary slogans. The Red Guards marched revisionist government officials through the streets with dunce caps on their heads. Cartoons attacking Liu and his policies went up all over China's major cities.

The Cultural Revolution had the desired political effect: by 1968 Liu's faction was purged from government control. Mao was back in power.

But he was faced with an unexpected side effect of the Revolution. With uncontrollable enthusiasm, the Red Guards continued their revolt. Still seeking out wrong-thinkers, Red Guard groups began to turn against each other as well as anyone who was not a Red Guard supporter. People were beaten up and sometimes killed by them.

Mao, Red Guards and Little Red Books.

Red Guards go on foot to carry the thoughts of Chairman Mao to the countryside.

Finally, Mao had to call on his ally Lin Biao. The People's Liberation Army came forward to put down the student revolt. In a single day of fighting in the grounds of Peking University, five students were killed and countless others injured. But China was eventually returned to an uneasy state of calm.

To counteract the revolutionary zeal of the students, Mao instructed them to look to the rural people of China in order to learn more about the real needs of their country. A new approach to education was established, in which students would spend a few months each year in the countryside, working on the land with the common people. In this way, Mao insured that the better educated would never come to feel themselves superior to the masses, and hard physical labour, helping to build up their country, would satisfy their need for social action.

Lin Biao's treachery

In Spring 1969, at the Ninth Congress of the Chinese Communist Party, Mao Tse-tung declared his "closest comrade in arms", Lin Biao, his successor as head of China. He thus acknowledged the debt he owed to the army leader for helping him through the ordeal of the Cultural Revolution.

It very soon became clear, however, that there were strong differences between the two leaders. Mao always believed that it was the people who ruled China; only through their support and action could advances be made. Lin, however, had supported Mao Tse-tung because he believed Mao had a unique genius for leading the Chinese people. In fact, Lin's

Lin Biao with the Little Red Book, which he was responsible for compiling.

thought was not very different from the elitist attitudes of Liu Shaoqi.

Lin naturally believed in himself as the unique leader to succeed Mao. When Mao became increasingly wary of Lin's attitudes and growing power, and started openly showing his disapproval, Lin began to make plans to insure his take-over of China.

In 1971 a plot was apparently devised to assassinate Mao Tse-tung. In September, Mao, on tour in China, visited Shanghai for conferences with local officials. His return journey to Peking would take him through Henan Province, where Lin's agents would blow up the Chairman's train.

No one is sure quite how this plot was foiled, but certainly, if it happened at all, it was foolhardy and poorly planned. Lin, his wife and son, and six of their fellow conspirators decided to flee to the Soviet Union. Although China kept quiet about the details of the incident, it appears that the aircraft that they commandeered crashed in Outer Mongolia, killing everyone on board. Over Peking Radio, Mao told the Chinese people his feelings about Lin's conspiracy. "What hurt and disappointed me most was the sinister arrow fired at my back by my ally."

Mao's last days

On 9th September 1976, Mao Tse-tung, China's Great Teacher, died in Peking at the age of 82. He had been ill for many months; photos and newsreels had shown him to be bowed with age, so feeble that he was barely able to hold up his head. Although it was not unexpected, Mao's death came as a shock to his people. The nation immediately plunged into eight days of mourning. Millions of Chinese filed past Mao's body in Peking's Great Hall of the People; many burst into tears at the sight of their dead leader.

Richard M. Nixon eating with Chou En-lai and greeting Mao.

65

Mao Tse-tung's final years had been active ones. They were marked most boldly by the way he and his trusted, able first minister Chou En-lai developed peaceful relations with their long-standing opponents, the United States.

After meeting head-on in Korea, China and the United States had again been adversaries in the war-torn southeast Asian country of Vietnam during the 1960s. The Chinese supported the Communist north of the country, which waged a Mao-style guerrilla war against the south, which was supported by American troops.

By 1971, it had become clear that the United States had no hope of winning the war in South Vietnam. In that year, too, Mao's China was finally accepted into the United Nations. It became more and more essential for the United States to establish its own relations with China, both for its own international standing and in the hope of reaching a solution to the Vietnam problem.

Mao in his seventies.

On 21st February 1972, President Richard Nixon arrived in Peking on an official visit to China. Within hours of his landing, Nixon came face-to-face with Mao Tse-tung in the book-lined study of Mao's home. Mao, with his simple good humour, put the President at ease. After a week of talks, China and the United States achieved a formal accord, agreeing that "No country should claim infallibility and each country should be prepared to re-examine its own attitudes for the common good." The way was paved for Chinese-American friendship, and this was one of the factors in the eventual U.S. withdrawal from the Vietnam war.

At home, Mao Tse-tung had to pave another political path. It was clear now that he did not have long to live. That made it even more essential for him to choose a successor. In April 1976, Mao's choice fell on Hua Guofeng, who was appointed first minister to fill the gap left by the death of Chou En-lai. Mao's will advised Hua to "act in line with past principles. With you in charge, I am at ease."

The Chinese political situation at Mao's death, however, was anything but easy. Jiang Qing, his widow, and three of her radical supporters in the government attempted to seize power from Hua, using a forged copy of Mao's will apparently doctored to endorse their leadership.

Chairman Hua began a political propaganda campaign against this "Gang of Four", as Jiang Qing and her supporters came to be called. All over China, hostile cartoons of Madame Mao and her supporters were posted, showing her as an empress luxuriating at the expense of China, as a

Mao's fourth wife, Jiang Qing.

Mao's successor, Hua Guofeng.

capitalist and as a vicious serpent. Within weeks of Hua's rise, the members of the "Gang of Four" were imprisoned. They were eventually placed on trial, and, in January 1981, two of them, including Jiang Qing, were condemned to death, although the sentence was suspended. In the intervening years, China changed course under its new leaders, who have moved away from Mao's brand of communism towards a new emphasis on technology and even the allowance of a limited degree of private enterprise. In the process, Mao's achievements have been looked at again, his mistakes have been acknowledged and more credit has been given to the other pioneer Chinese Communists.

There can be little doubt that China in the future will experience further turmoil. Mao knew it would happen. Although he had wrought immense changes in the brief span of a few decades, it would take much longer than that to change a nation and a people with a past that goes back thousands of years. What was important was that Mao had brought communism to China. With that knowledge, Mao was at least certain in himself that China's future would be bright. This passionate belief he expressed in the last poem he ever wrote, just a year before he died:

Loyal parents who sacrificed so much for the nation
Never feared the ultimate fate.
Now that our country has become red
Who will be its guardian?
Our mission, unfinished, may take a thousand years.
The struggle tires us, and our hair is grey.
You and I, old friends, can we just watch our efforts be washed away?

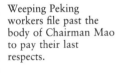

Weeping Peking workers file past the body of Chairman Mao to pay their last respects.

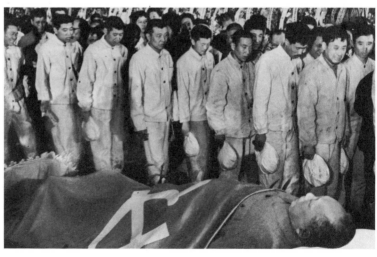

Chronology

This list of dates gives the main events in the life of Mao Tse-tung together with a few of the many other things that were happening in the world at the time and are not mentioned elsewhere in this book. Events in bold type are covered in the main text of the book.

1893 **Birth of Mao Tse-tung.**
1894 **China declares war on Japan.**
1895 First public film show. Wilhelm Röntgen discovers X-rays.
1898 Spanish-American War. Pierre and Marie Curie discover radium.
1899 Start of Boer War in South Africa (ends 1902).
1900 Boxer Rising against Europeans in China. Sigmund Freud's book *The Interpretation of Dreams.*
1901 Death of Queen Victoria. Assassination of President McKinley. Guglielmo Marconi transmits messages by wireless telegraphy across Atlantic.
1903 Wilbur and Orville Wright make first flight in heavier-than-air machine.
1904 Russo-Japanese war (ends 1905).
1910 **Mao goes to Xiangxiang.** Japan formally annexes Korea.
1911 **Mao arrives in Changsha.** Sun Yat-sen proclaimed President of Chinese Republic.
1912 **Mao enrols in Teacher Training College. Yuan Shikai becomes Chinese President.**
1913 Sun Yat-sen's United League becomes the Guomindang (GMD). Warlord activity in China. Opening of Panama Canal.
1914 Start of World War I.
1915 Einstein's General Theory of Relativity. **Yuan Shikai becomes Chinese Emperor.**
1916 **Death of Yuan Shikai.** Easter Rising in Dublin.
1917 **Mao publishes his first article.** USA declares war on Germany. March (liberal) and October (Bolshevik) revolutions in Russia.
1918 **Mao graduates and goes to Peking.** End of World War I.
1919 **Mao founds** *Xiang River Review.* **Student demonstrations in Peking (May 4th movement).** Versailles Peace Conference. First transatlantic flight.
1920 **Mao marries Yang Kaihui.** League of Nations founded.
1921 **Foundation of Chinese Communist Party (CCP).**
1922 Benito Mussolini sets up Fascist government in Italy.
1923 **CCP alliance with GMD; Mao represents CCP on GMD committee.**
1925 **Mao falls ill and returns to Shaoshan.** Sun Yat-sen dies; succeeded by Chiang Kai-shek.
1926 **Chiang launches Northern Expedition.** General Strike in Britain.
1927 **Massacre of communists in Shanghai. Autumn Harvest Uprising in Hunan.**
1928 **GMD forces take Peking. Chiang becomes Chinese President.**
1929 Wall Street Crash starts Great Depression.
1930 **Communists attack Changsha. Execution of Yang Kaihui. Jiangxi Soviet set up.**
1931 Japanese occupy Manchuria.
1933 **Chiang starts massive blockade of Jiangxi Soviet.**

Adolf Hitler becomes German Chancellor. New Deal in USA.
1934 **Start of Long March from Jiangxi.**
1935 **Long March ends in Shaanxi.**
1936 **Yanan becomes capital of Chinese Soviet Republic. Chiang kidnapped by Zhang Zueliang. Alliance of CCP and GMD against Japanese.** Abdication of Edward VIII. Start of Spanish Civil War (ends 1939). First television service (BBC, London).
1937 **Mao divorced from He Zizhen. First battles between GMD and Japanese.**
1938 Germany annexes Austria. Munich conference.
1939 **Mao marries Jiang Qing.** Britain and France declare war on Germany: start of World War II.
1941 Lend-Lease system of US aid for Britain. German invasion of USSR. Japanese bombing of Pearl Harbor brings USA into war.
1944 D-Day: Allied landings in Normandy, France.
1945 **Meeting of Mao and Chiang.** Yalta conference. Death of Roosevelt. Surrender of Germany and suicide of Hitler. Atom bombs dropped on Hiroshima and Nagasaki. Surrender of Japan ends World War II.
1946 **Civil war in China.** First meeting of United Nations (UN) General Assembly.
1947 Truman Doctrine of aid to countries threatened by communism. Independence for India and Pakistan.
1948 Jewish government formed in Israel. *Apartheid* becomes government policy in South Africa. Communist government formed in North Korea. Berlin airlift combats Russian blockade.
1949 **People's Republic of China founded.**
1950 **Mao meets Stalin in Moscow. War in Korea.**
1953 Armistice in Korea. First Five Year Plan in China.
1956 **Mao's first Yangtze swim. Start of Hundred Flowers movement.** Suez crisis and Arab-Israeli War. Hungarian revolution put down by Russia.
1957 Treaty of Rome establishes European Common Market. Russians launch first two Sputnik space satellites.
1958 **The Great Leap Forward.**
1959 Communist government under Fidel Castro in Cuba.
1960 **Soviet aid withdrawn from China. Mao resigns as Chairman.**
1961 Berlin Wall seals East-West border. Yuri Gargarin becomes first man in space.
1962 Cuban missile crisis.
1963 Nuclear test ban treaty. Assassination of President Kennedy.
1964 **Publication of** *The Thoughts of Chairman Mao.* War in South Vietnam involves USA.
1965 Americans bomb North Vietnam. Unilateral Declaration of Independence in Rhodesia.
1966 **Mao's second Yangtze swim. Cultural Revolution in China.**
1967 Six Day War between Israel and Arabs.
1968 Soviet invasion of Czechoslovakia.
1969 **Lin Biao declared Mao's successor.** Neil Armstrong first man to land on moon.
1971 **Lin Biao killed in air crash after plot to assassinate Mao. China accepted as member of UN.**
1972 **President Nixon meets Mao in Peking.**
1973 US forces withdraw from Vietnam.
1974 Resignation of President Nixon.
1976 **Death of Mao.**

Index

Page numbers in italic indicate picture captions

Borodin, Mikhail *31*

Changsha 7, 10, 13, 17, 18, 20, 21, 24, 27, 29, 37, 38, 39
Chen Duxiu 28, 29
Chiang Kai-shek 34, *35, 35,* 37–40, 42, 48–54, *48, 50, 51*
Chongqing 49, *51*
Chou En-lai 48, *50,* 56, 65, 66
Ci Xi, Dowager Empress 7
Clear Water Pool House 29, 38
Communist Party of China 26, 28, 30–32, 35, 38, 42, 53–55, 58, 59, 60
Confucius 7, 10, 16, 26
Communes 60, *60*
Co-operatives 57, 60
Cultural Revolution 63, *63*

Dadu River 42, 43

Eighth Route Army 49
Emperor 6, 13, 14, 16, 18, 19

Formosa *see* Taiwan
France 24, 26

Gang of Four 66, 67
Guomindang Party 22, 30, 31, *31,* 32, 34–44, 49, 51, 52, 54

He Zizhen *,46*
Hua Guofeng 66, 67
Hunan province 6, 8, *11,* 13, *14,* 28, 29, 30, 33, 38

Japan *12,* 13, 16, 18, 22, 26, 27, 47, 48, 49, *49,* 50, 55
Jiang Qing 52, 53, 62, 66, 67

Jiangxi province 36, 37, 40
Jiangxi Soviet 37, 39, 40

Korean War 55, 66
Khrushchev, Nikita 61

Lenin, V.I. 31
Li Dazhao 24, 25, 28
Lin Biao 36, 37, 61, 62, *62,* 64, 65, *65*
Little Red Book 6–63, *63,* 65
Liu Shaoqi 56, 61, 62, 63, 65
Long March 40–46, *41,* 52
Luding Bridge 43, *43*

Macarthur, General Douglas 55
Mao Anqing *38*
Mao Anying 38, 55, *55*
Mao Rensheng 7–11, 14, *15,* 25
Mao Tse-tung (pictures) *5, 21, 22, 23, 33, 36, 37, 40, 42, 46, 50, 51, 53, 55, 56, 60, 61, 62, 66, 67*
Mao Zemin 23, 31, *39*
Mao Zetan 23, *39*
Marco Polo Bridge 49
Marx, Karl 25, *25,* 28, 33

New People's Study Society 24, 27, 29
Nixon, Richard M. 65, 66

Pearl Harbor 50
Peking 13, 22, 24, 25, 27, 28, 34, 35, 49, 53, 62, 64, 65
People's Liberation Army 52, *52,* 53, 55, 61, 64
People's Republic of China 53, *53,* 54–67, 57
Red Army (Chinese) 36–42, 44–46, *45,* 47, 49, 52, 61
Red Guards 63, *63,* 64
Russia 25, 31, 54, 55, 56, 58–61

Shanghai 26–30, 35, *35,* 49, 65
Shaanxi Province 45, 47, 49, 52

Shaoshan 7, 8, 9, 14, 15, 24, 32, *33*
Socialist Youth Corps 29
Soong Ching-ling 30, 47
Soong Mei-ling 47
Stalin, Joseph 54, 55, *55,* 61
Sun Yat-sen 17–19, *17, 19,* 22, 30, *30,* 31, 34, *34*

Taiwan 13, 53, 54
Tibet 45
Trade Unions 27, 29

United League 17–19, 22
United Nations 66
United States 18, 22, 50, 66

Versailles Treaty 26, 27
Vietnam 66

Water Margin, The 11, 14
Wen Jimei 9–10, 15, 23, 24
World War I 22, 26
World War II 50, 55

Xiang River 17, 41
Xiang River Daily News 19
Xiang River Review 27, 28
Xiangdan 15
Xiangxiang 15, 16

Yanan 47, 48, 50, 52, 53
Yang Changzhi 21–24
Yang Kaihui 21, 25, *25,* 28–30, 38, *38, 39*
Yangtze River 18, 42, 58, 62, *62*
Yuan Shikai 19, *19,* 22
Yunnan Province 42

Zhang Jingyao 28, 29
Zhang Xueliang 48, *48*
Zhang Zuolin 34
Zhu De 36, 37, 42, *56*

Books to Read

This list includes some of the many books in which you can read more about Mao Tse-Tung and China. The names of the British and American publishers and the date of first publication are given after each title.

Mao Tse-Tung Stuart Schram (Pelican/Simon & Schuster 1966, 1973)

Mao: The People's Emperor Dick Wilson (Hutchinson/Doubleday 1979)

Mao Tse-Tung John Robotham (Making of the Modern World series, Longmans 1974)

Mao Tse-Tung H. Purcell (Wayland/St Martin's Press 1977)

The Morning Deluge, Mao Tse-Tung and the Chinese Revolution 1893-1953 Han Suyin (Cape/Little, Brown 1972)

Wind in the Tower, Mao Tse-Tung and the Chinese Revolution 1949-1975 Han Suyin (Cape/Little, Brown 1976)

Mao Tse-Tung Unrehearsed edited by Stuart Schram (Penguin/Pantheon 1974)

Mao and the Chinese Revolution Jerome Ch'en (Oxford University Press paperback, 1968)

Mao Tse-Tung and China C. P. Fitzgerald (Hodder & Stoughton/Homes & Meier 1976)

The Long March Dick Wilson (Hamish Hamilton/Viking 1971)

The Fall of Shanghai: The Communist Take-Over in 1949 Noel Barber (Macmillan/Coward McCann 1979)

China (Macdonald Countries Special/Silver Burdett 1979)

The Chinese: A Portrait David Bonavia (Allen Lane/Harper & Row 1980)